# YOU
## ARE THE
## FIRST
# YOU

# YOU
## ARE THE
# FIRST
# YOU

## WHITNEY
## HOLTZMAN

*You Are the First You*

Edited by Liesel Schmidt and Regina Cornell
Cover design by Robin Vuchnich
Cover Photography by Andi Diamond
Interior design by Nikkita Kent

Indigo River Publishing
3 West Garden Street, Ste. 718
Pensacola, FL 32502
www.indigoriverpublishing.com

Ordering Information:
Special discounts are available on quantity purchases by corporations, associations, and others. For details, contact the publisher at the address above.

Orders by US trade bookstores and wholesalers: Please contact the publisher at the address above.

Printed in the United States of America
LCCN: 2020930234
ISBN: 978-1-950906-46-8 (paperback), 978-1-950906-47-5 (ebook)

First edition

*With Indigo River Publishing, you can always expect great books, strong voices, and meaningful messages.*
*Most importantly, you'll always find . . .* words worth reading.

*"People will forget what you said, people will forget what you did, but people will never forget how you made them feel."*

—Maya Angelou

If you take one lesson away from this book, I hope it's that you remember that people will never forget how you make them feel.

# CONTENTS

# CHAPTER 1

## TEN YEARS IN THE MAKING

When my dad, Steve, was in seventh grade, he wrote an essay about his dream to live in a New York City high-rise and enjoy life as a bachelor. He grew up in a small town, idolizing the Yankees and admiring the players' heroic status and chic, carefree lifestyles in the big city.

Clearly, kids weren't exactly in the life picture my dad was painting for himself, and at this point, my arrival seemed far from promising.

Cue Gail Golman.

When Steve met my mom, Gail, she told him that, unfortunately, they couldn't date seriously because he didn't envision having kids. He pondered her statement, called her back, and told her he would agree to have one child. She informed him that my dad's proposed compromise wouldn't do the trick. Gail wanted at least two kids, and she wasn't budging. He phoned again and said okay, he would agree to have two children. And thus began their long-term marriage. Ten years in, I came along, followed by my brother, Josh, three years later. A miniature poodle, Casey, later joined the mix, as well.

But let's start at the beginning.

My mom is from Chicago, and my dad is from a town in upstate New York called Elmira, but he'd moved to Chicago by the time they met. They got married when my mom was twenty-five and my dad was twenty-six, after having been set up on a blind date and knowing each other for only seven months. On one of their early dates, when my mom went over to my dad's apartment, she mentioned that she liked the furniture. He said, "It's from the roof!" My dad had borrowed his building's patio furniture to decorate his apartment and impress her. He'd also told her the first date was casual. She showed up (he didn't have a car, so she had to drive), and he was standing at the front doorway in a three-piece suit. He then asked her to look in the closet and help him pick out an outfit. At the restaurant, when my dad ordered one salad for them to split, Gail drew a line down the middle, making sure she got exactly half of the salad.

A love of food runs in the family, as the Holtzmans rarely miss a meal. In fact, years later, my mom sent my brother and me to a class to learn about manners and etiquette. I came home crying hysterically. When my mom asked what could possibly have been so upsetting at a manners class, I replied, "The teacher told us it's not polite to ask for seconds on a date."

My worst nightmare.

When my parents discussed getting engaged, my dad said to my mom, "I didn't think you were the type of woman who wanted a ring." My mom set the record straight, and luckily, he had a ring by the time the proposal came along. He never made that mistake again.

After getting married, my mom was ready to have kids right away. She'll tell you she was meant to be a mom, but my dad wasn't ready for kids yet. Gail was an English teacher at the time, and my favorite anecdote from those days is the time she had a mouse in her classroom. Apparently, she stood on her desk and screamed until someone came and took care of the rodent.

Since my dad wasn't ready to have kids, my mom, at twenty-nine years old, decided to go to law school, where, hopefully, she'd encounter fewer rodents. Ironically, she now lives an hour from a mouse named Mickey. More than thirty years after that decision to go to law school, she's a total Boss Lady and one of the top lawyers in the country.

After moving to Tampa, Florida, in 1986 to be with my mom's sister and her family, my parents finally decided they were ready for kids. I was the first to arrive, born on June 23, 1987. My due date was actually June 6, but my mom finally went into labor on Father's Day, June 21. She thought, *How great! We'll have a baby on Father's Day!* Turns out, I didn't arrive for two more days (after many hours of labor), until June 23. I'm still a homebody to this day! For anyone who knows me, my birthday is my favorite day of the year, and I celebrate it as such. Years later, when I went to work at VaynerMedia, an employee's birthday was considered a holiday there. I knew I'd found my people!

I was also born into the best family I could imagine. I may be biased, but Gail and Steve are the most loving parents and the best people I know. The greatest gift you can give anyone in your life is to allow them to be exactly who they are, and they always gave us that permission. As the greatest boss and teacher I've ever had, Gary Vaynerchuk, says, "Why do we love our parents? It's because they loved us first." If you're in any position of authority, the way to earn love and respect from those around you is to genuinely show it to them first. My parents did that, and I will always be grateful to them for their unconditional love.

My mom attended temple board meetings on Monday nights when my brother and I were growing up, and on those nights, she gave my dad one assignment: "Make sure the kids are in bed when I get home." After every board meeting in the fall, she would come home, and my dad would be sitting on the couch with one arm around me and his other arm around my brother—all of us watching *Monday Night Football* together. Of course, we were still awake. My dad refers to those Monday nights as "quality parenting."

When family and friends came to our house when I was young, the first item I would show them on our house tour was the time-out chair. It was a really comfortable peach-colored chair that spun around. It was also where I spent a lot of my time growing up.

My parents often say I was a good kid, but I liked to push the limits. I've told them that my pushing the limits was just me being entrepreneurial—they just misbranded it! I truly believe that if I hadn't pushed the limits, I wouldn't have a business today.

If you look back over my childhood, you'll see those glimmers of precociousness that really played into my success as an adult and the way I still think. Case in point: When I was approximately three years old, my cousin Benjamin would test me on the names of baseball players. He would say the first name, and I had to recite the player's last name. For example, he would say, "Mickey," and I would say, "Mantle." When he got to Cecil (referring to Cecil Fielder), I said, "Harassment!" I think that, even at age three, I had already spent too many years listening to my mom, a labor and employment lawyer, on her calls talking about sexual harassment cases. My brother, Josh, included that anecdote as part of his application to Harvard Law School (he got in). His point was that law had been in the family and in his DNA all along. I, on the other hand, recall family dinners talking about the law, and I knew even then that a monotonous work routine on a daily basis wouldn't work for my soul. I had no idea at the time that my mind-set was called entrepreneurial, but I couldn't understand how a person could go to work and not have each day be filled with surprises and exciting moments.

I was a pistol as a child. Around age three, I decided to do a somersault in the middle of ballet. What can I say—the class needed a little spicing up. The teacher, Miss Lou, informed my mom that somersaults were not allowed in ballet class. Soon after, I was enrolled in gymnastics. It was clear early on that I had a lot of energy and my own way of doing things.

Around age four, I had a discussion with my mom where I expressed that I felt my one-year-old brother was standing too close to the pool. I wouldn't relent on my stance, as I feared for his safety. I eventually won, and she moved him away from the pool. By age eight,

I helped to plan my birthday parties and book my own camp reservations. I became independent very early on because I had two working parents.

I had an ideal childhood in Tampa, growing up with a very close family. I went to a prestigious preparatory school in the area. When I started third grade, I met a teacher who had a high EQ, or emotional intelligence, and a heart of gold. She understood me, and, it turns out, she was another woman who also loved sports. Mrs. Kathy Gruden, whose husband and sons coached in the NFL, was the first and only teacher I had in school who ever taught me about sports. I will never forget that 7 x 7 = 49ers, because of Mrs. Gruden. She really knew how to teach multiplication!

In fourth grade, I was called down to the principal's office. Typically, if you were in trouble—worst-case scenario—you saw the elementary school director. The fact that I was being called down to see the head of the entire school made me think something serious had happened—maybe a death in the family. Turns out, the principal wanted me to teach him how to book plane reservations on Expedia. He'd heard that I had mastered making travel plans online, which was still an anomaly at the time.

When I was in school, I truly didn't know what my strengths were or what I was meant to do in the world. I felt like I was the odd girl out growing up, like I didn't relate to the kids around me. What I learned later is that that feeling often means you're meant for greatness and your own unique path. You just can't see it at the time, when you're in the midst of it all and comparing yourself to your peers. When I went back to speak at my former school years later, a student asked me if I had always been entrepreneurial. I laughed and said, "They only call it that when it works!" At the time, however, you're thought of as a disappointment for not staying on track with the other kids.

I've learned that it's essential to have an unwavering belief in yourself and tunnel vision for what you're meant for in the world. You have to tune out all the doubters, even the ones close to you. You cannot allow the fears of others, who want to steer you toward a traditional path, to derail you from the greatness for which you are meant.

Always an ambitious student, I worked hard and earned As and Bs. I was mature beyond my years and didn't know my place in the world. And I was that kid on the playground befriending the little girl standing alone, the friend to kids who didn't have one. Very early on, it was clear I was an empath.

As the school years progressed, and I made my way through high school, I knew I had two passions: sports and current events. It wasn't until I started college that I realized I could segue those interests into a major: sports journalism. When I didn't want to study or do homework in high school, watching football was my escape.

We would be so much better off as a society if we put kids on a path early on that played to their strengths. Instead of saying that success is getting As in these four subjects, we should test kids to find out what they're good at and have them take classes that fit their specific skill sets. Instead of generations of kids growing up thinking they don't fit in and then rebelling, our society would allow kids to grow up with self-esteem and a belief in the person they are meant to be. After all, *you are the first you.*

I have no doubt my love of sports came from my dad. He's a diehard New York Yankees fan and was the lawyer for the group who brought the Tampa Bay Lightning to our hometown. In addition to our nights together watching *Monday Night Football* (while I was supposed to be sleeping), my childhood Sundays were spent with my dad at the Tampa Bay Buccaneers' games. I remember getting so emotional about the final outcomes that I'd hide in the bathroom during close games. I was so excited when the Bucs finally won their first Super Bowl that I made a scrapbook with photos and news clippings from the season, including a minute-by-minute itinerary of their Super Bowl Week timeline.

I often say I grew up in Tampa at the perfect time to form a love of sports. In addition to what was fostered at home, Tampa was awarded NHL and MLB franchises during my childhood, the Bucs won their first Super Bowl, and the Rays earned their first World Series berth. The Tampa sports world and I grew up together, hand in hand. Those joyful moments helped shape my life at such a formative age, in ways I could never have imagined at the time.

During my early middle school years, I lost my remaining three grandparents within a year and a half of each other (as if middle school isn't already hard enough). In March of 2000, my dad's father suffered a heart attack in Boston's Logan Airport and unexpectedly passed away. My mom's father fell ill with an autoimmune disease right around the same time, and my mom went back and forth to Chicago to be with him. While he was in a coma, my grandmother, his wife, was diagnosed out of nowhere with pancreatic cancer and passed away a few days later in September of 2000. Approximately one year after losing his wife, my mom's father succumbed to his autoimmune illness in October of 2001. My middle school years were straight chaos.

Those experiences were my first run-in with tragedy, as I was close to all of them. They were like second parents to me and came down to Tampa to visit all the time. A year after that two-year ordeal with my grandparents, my aunt Franci, my mom's sister, was diagnosed with ovarian cancer at the age of fifty-three. I was very close to her, as our birthdays were a week apart and we had similar personalities. She lived a mile down the road from me growing up and became a second mom to me. Franci Rudolph lived such an impactful life that she has a number of legacies honoring her in Tampa. The mayor even spoke at her funeral. I'd sit with her in the cancer ward and realize how lucky we are on the days we get to be at home, feeling bored, because it means we have our health and our family. If you have those two factors, you have everything you need in life.

At a fragile age I learned from those family members that life is short. I wanted each of my days to be worthwhile and to have a career that I loved. There was only one answer: sports.

## CHAPTER LESSONS

- People will never forget how you made them feel.
- The best gift you can give anyone in your life is to allow them to be exactly who they are.
- Why do we love our parents? They loved us first (a famous Gary Vaynerchuk lesson).
- They only call it entrepreneurial once it works.
- You have to tune out all the doubters and have an unwavering belief in yourself.
- If you have your health and family, you have everything you need in life.

# CHAPTER 2

# THE BLACK SHEEP OR THE ONE WHO GOT AWAY?

Both of my parents are lawyers, and my brother is also. I'm still not sure whether I'm the black sheep or the one who got away.

When I entered college and told my parents I wanted to be the sideline reporter on *Monday Night Football*, they asked if I could pick a job with more than one opening. I replied, "Sure! I'll also do *Sunday Night Football*, which just doubled my options!" They probably thought they'd have to support me for the rest of my life.

At the prep school I went to growing up, every kid's first word was basically "Harvard." There was—and still is—an emphasis on getting a great education at the school, which means that kids are dreaming big academically from a young age. So I thought I must attend an Ivy League school or an institution of the same caliber in order to be successful. Let me just say that I learned throughout the college process that happiness equals success. If you're in a place where your heart is happy and your soul is thriving, you're going to be successful.

It's also important to find a school that matches your interests. I wanted to major in sports broadcasting, so a big football powerhouse was always going to be a better fit for me than a school where no one knew if there was even a game that day.

When I began the college search process, I visited a prestigious Division III school in the Midwest. As we walked by the football stadium during my official tour of the campus, I saw a small number of fans in the stands. Thinking I might be missing something, I said to the tour guide, "Your intramural program looks great, but where is your actual football stadium?" The tour guide said, "Oh, that *is* our real football team." I probably had the most alarmed look on my face. In that moment, I knew I needed to do an about-face and find a school with a big football program.

When I refocused my search, listening to what my heart wanted, I ended up applying to the University of Florida, the University of Texas, and Florida State. I wanted a big school in a warm climate (I hate being cold), with a great sports program and other Jewish students.

The minute I stepped foot onto the University of Florida's campus, I knew it was where I belonged. With its brick buildings, UF looked exactly like my vision of a college campus, plus it was only a two-hour drive from my home in Tampa. Luckily, Florida has a scholarship program, called Bright Futures, that assists college students with tuition if they achieved a certain GPA in high school and a certain SAT/ACT score. I didn't realize it until many years later, during my job at MLB, but what a gift it was to not have to pay tuition. Life is expensive enough as it is, and I looked around at my coworkers, thinking, *Wow, we're all at the same company, but so many of these people are going to have years of student loan debt.*

For what I wanted out of a college experience, I couldn't have made a better choice. From the time I was accepted into UF until the time I graduated, the Gators won two basketball titles and two football titles. Talk about a dynasty! I was also a student there at the same time as Tim Tebow andI was able to interview him because I was a sports reporter for the campus TV station, WUFT. People often say to me, "You were there at a great time." To which I always reply: "All I'm saying is that I got there, they got good. I graduated, and the teams went downhill. So I'm not saying I had anything to do with it, but you can't ignore the facts!" What can I say? We won championships together. It was an epic run in college sports that's unlikely to be matched.

My dad worked for the SEC (Securities and Exchange Commission), so I like to say that the SEC runs in my DNA, even though my version of the SEC is the Southeastern Conference. It still feels like a bond we share, and the SEC was destined to be my fate.

College was really the first place I saw my discipline separate me from the pack. I don't suffer from FOMO, otherwise known as fear of missing out. I'm extremely directed, and I know what I'm meant for in life. I had very big dreams. I didn't want to be like every other kid out there, so why would I feel the need to do exactly what they were doing?

I spent every summer of college using my time wisely with internships and gave a lot of effort to my schoolwork and building my career. That hard work really gave me a leg up when I graduated, because I already had real-world experience on my résumé. Everyone wants to be the second person to give you a job. It's much more difficult to land your first job, so getting a head start with work experience in college really gives you a competitive edge when you're applying for your first job out of school.

I remember many nights when my friends were going out while I was in my dorm or the sorority house, applying for internships. There's no replacement for doing the actual work.

Discipline set me apart from my peers in college, and as I've gone about life, I've seen it be the differentiating factor between those who succeed and those who don't fulfill their potential. Mental strength allows you to go all in on what you're meant for, which means that the dividends will really pay off in those categories. If, however, you're weak and easily give in to temptation, you'll likely end up dipping a toe in a bunch of different ponds but never investing the necessary effort to reach your dreams. Simply put: discipline separates the winners from the losers. You cannot have success without being disciplined.

Speaking of discipline . . . My college friends knew not to come into my room from four to five p.m. because that was the sacred time I spent watching *Oprah* every day. I often refer to Oprah as my "Bible", and I just know that she and I would be best friends—if she knew I existed. Oprah was the first person I could spend day after day and year after year with who had an extraordinarily high emotional intelligence. I still didn't truly know what that term meant, but what I *did* know was that Oprah understood the world the same way I did, asked questions I wanted to know the answers to, and allowed me into a world every day that really resonated with me. She was getting to know people and telling their stories. I was drawn to that above all else.

I clearly remember one particular afternoon at the sorority house when something finally clicked for me. I was lying in bed, the UF band was practicing outside my window, and my best friend Oprah was on the TV. Oprah said something to a guest that I will never forget. She said, "I always knew I was meant for greatness." I sat up immediately in bed because it was the first time someone had ever explained exactly how my soul felt. I could never verbalize it before she uttered those words, but that was the same feeling I've always had within me.

The year I graduated college, 2010, coincided with *Oprah*'s last season on air. My aunt and uncle in Chicago surprised me with tickets to see her show live—the definition of a bucket-list item of mine coming true, as getting to see her show live had been one of my greatest dreams. Since it was her last season, the tickets came through just in time. My cousin Randell, who is four days older than I am, and I arrived at Harpo Studios very early in the morning the day of the show. We weren't told what the episode was about ahead of time or who the guests would be, so we were in for an adventure. Our first stop in the studio was a big, gym-like room that was filled with nail stations. Apparently, we were getting our nails painted before going into the live taping. *That's it!* I thought. *We're winning diamond rings, and they want our nails to look nice! How thoughtful of Oprah!*

Once we took our seats (we were seated in the VIP area and had been told to wear bright colors because we would most likely be on TV), Oprah came out before the taping and began schmoozing with the audience. Like. A. Regular. Person. She was just as amazing as I imagined, because her heart of gold was *real*. She took a few questions before the show, and a student raised her hand and told Oprah she loved her magazine and couldn't wait to subscribe one day, but she currently couldn't afford the cost of the subscription as a student. Oprah immediately called her team out into the audience to take down the girl's information and gave her a subscription on the house. And this was *before* the cameras began rolling.

Our episode ended up being about celebrities who were planning for the next phase of their careers once their current celebrity roles came to an end. One of the guests was Serena Williams, who was enrolled in classes to become a nail technician. Serena had partnered with OPI to create her own line of nail polishes.

All I heard Oprah say was, "You're all winning free . . ."

So, naturally, I completely lost it. My hero and best friend was about to give ME a gift. And if you ever watched *Oprah*, you know she did it big. So I assumed a plane, a house, a trip around the world . . . or even that diamond ring for which she'd had our nails painted.

Turns out the answer was nail polish.

We all got a free set of Serena's colors. But it was too late. I'd already lost it when I heard that Oprah was giving me a gift. So while everyone else was clapping politely in the background, the cameras went straight to my face because I was completely ecstatic—clapping and cheering with the biggest smile on my face you could ever imagine. It looked like she'd just given me a car. To this day, it's still a joke in my family about how I reacted to a few bottles of OPI nail polish.

Aside from my hours of investing in *Oprah* paying off at the end of my college career, so, too, did the internship experience I gained while I was at UF.

I interned for the Tampa Bay Rays, Turner Sports, and ESPN during my three summers of college. It was really those summers and using my time wisely that set me apart from my peers career-wise.

My first internship in sports was with the Tampa Bay Rays, between my freshman and sophomore years of college, in 2007. I felt very fortunate to land a job with my hometown team, which had arrived in Tampa when I was growing up. My role was as a stadium operations intern. On game days, I worked from about ten a.m. until the last fan left the stadium, including weekends and holidays. I was also in charge of calling in spills—"Soda cleanup on the stairs of section 110, row A"—and making sure the fans had a safe and enjoyable experience during their time at Tropicana Field. I was also in charge of letting our operations team know when there was an egress of people leaving after the game, so they could prepare for the rush. I clearly recall once relaying an egress over the radio, and then a teammate came on the system and asked where the *egret* was.

It wasn't exactly my dream job, but I felt grateful to have my first opportunity in the sports world. I was also grateful that my role in the stadium operations department only lasted three months. Internships are a great way to figure out what you *don't* want to do. While I loved the Rays organization and being in the middle of the MLB action, I was able to use the experience to know that stadium operations wasn't the best fit for my personality. However, that role with the Rays opened so many doors. With your first job or internship, you can't be picky, and you have to cast your net wide. During my summer with the Rays, the organization was changing its name from the Devil Rays to the Rays, so I was able to watch the rebranding of a major sports franchise right in front of my eyes. You also don't have the foresight to know when an experience is going to come back and pay off down the road.

One of my personal *SportsCenter* highlights took place while I was interning for the Rays. The team hosted a soda bottle race in the middle of the game, where Pepsi, Sierra Mist, and Aquafina mascots all raced to a finish line at home plate. Without my knowing, my fellow interns signed me up for one of these races. I felt like this could be my shining moment, so I got my parents tickets to the game so that they could see me race in person.

I was the Aquafina bottle that night. First of all, I kept forgetting I was in a bottle. So as I walked to the field for the race, everyone was yelling comments at me. I kept smiling back, totally forgetting I was in a bottle costume and that the fans couldn't see my face and smiles.

The race didn't quite go as planned, either.

When you're a mascot, they don't fit the shoes to your feet, and the costume is the size it is—basically a one-size-fits-all approach. Well, the shoes were like a size 12, or something way too big for my feet. I didn't really realize this conundrum until I was about to start the race. So as we took off in front of a stadium of fans, I was moving at a very slow pace, just trying to keep the shoes on my feet. I finished so far behind that I'm pretty sure the race ended before I crossed the finish line. The Rays were playing the White Sox that day, and as I walked off the field, one of the players said to me, "You looked really flat out there," trying to make a soda joke. It's a good thing that performance isn't on video anywhere.

My next summer of college, 2008, I interned for Turner Sports in Atlanta as a production intern. I was getting closer to my passion. The following fall, the Rays made it to their first World Series. Turns out TBS, owned by Turner, broadcast the American League Championship Series (the ALCS), and the Rays were one of the two contenders, which ultimately earned them a berth in the World Series. Both of my internships had just united. I called my former boss at Turner to ask if they needed help during the ALCS. I was back at UF, only two hours away, and could easily drive back to the Tampa area for the games. He told me they were actually in need of a runner, someone who could help the production team run errands. I told him I was in, and I drove back and forth to St. Petersburg from Gainesville for the games at Tropicana Field, which luckily fell on the weekends.

In addition to running errands, my role was to drive the broadcasters, Ron Darling, Buck Martinez, and Chip Caray, to and from their hotel for the games. While these three famous guys probably would've preferred to be in a limo versus a Jeep Cherokee with a college kid as their driver, they could not have been kinder, more gracious, or more supportive. We often chatted during our drives over the bridge, and they became like family by the end of the Series. I will never forget those three guys' characters. They didn't even have to talk to me, but they still made me feel like an equal. In fact, Buck gave me two tickets to one of the final ALCS games so that my parents could come and enjoy a game. My heart was so full, being able to give my parents a gift that would blow them away.

All the runners wore very relaxed clothes, but I'm a big believer in putting my best forward. When everyone else goes left, you go right. That's how you stand out. So every day I was at the ALCS, while my fellow runners were in clothes you'd wear to the gym, I got dressed as if I were an executive, not a runner. As the old adage goes, "Dress for the job you want, not the job you have." One day, as I was standing at the entrance to the field, a gentleman started talking to me. He was so kind and a wonderful conversationalist. He spent many minutes asking all about me, wanting to know where I went to school and about my career path so far. After he'd spent ample time getting to know me, I finally asked him what he did. Turns out that his name was Jonathan Mariner, and he was the CFO of Major League Baseball. I think my jaw hit the ground because this high-level executive had just spent so long making me feel important and special. Not only is Jonathan still one of my mentors, that fateful interaction and the choices I made leading up to it impacted my life in ways I could never have imagined in that moment.

Later down the road, when I worked for MLB, I was sent to the Rays' spring training, where I met team owner Stu Sternberg. I would never have had a good reason to approach Stu had I not interned with the Rays years earlier. When I was in that Aquafina bottle costume in 2007, I would've never expected I'd be standing near the team owner years later and that that summer would give us common ground to get to know one another. Ultimately, I was able to help connect his family friend, who was just coming out of college at the time, to the right person in my MLB social media department to land a job. It was nice to do a small favor for Stu in return and to continue to build a relationship. After college, when I worked for espnW, I came back to interview Melanie Lenz, the Rays' chief development officer and the highest-ranking woman in the organization. Now that I live back in

Tampa, many of the employees I met in that first role are my sports colleagues and neighbors.

It never ceases to amaze me how an experience that may seem meaningless at the time can pay off years later. Always put your best foot forward. You never know who's watching and how a connection you make will come back to benefit you down the road.

## CHAPTER LESSONS

- Happiness = Success
- Go, Gators! Always.
- Be disciplined. Do not give in to temptation that will derail your dreams.
- There is no replacement for doing the actual work.
- Internships are the best way to learn what you *don't* want to do.
- For your first job or internship, cast your net wide. You can be pickier as time goes on, after you gain more experience.
- When everyone else goes left, you go right.

# CHAPTER 3

# ESPNol

During my junior year of college, ESPN came to UF to recruit interns. After working in production the previous summer at Turner and my prior experience in the sports world, I knew ESPN would be the pinnacle of internships for me. And if you haven't noticed yet, I tend to dream big. Like pretty much the top.

To set the scene, Tim Tebow was the reigning Heisman Trophy winner. He was the first sophomore player ever to win the trophy when he did so the previous season, in 2007, so we were already on the heels of an unprecedented sports year at UF. On September 27, 2008, Tebow delivered his passionate "I Promise" speech, in which he promised to work harder than any other player had ever worked, and he willed the team to another national football title at the end of the 2008 season, in the middle of my junior year.

So, by the time ESPN came to recruit on the University of Florida's campus, the Gators were IT in terms of being the center of the sports world. I have been very fortunate in my life that timing has played a role in my dreams coming true. Similar to how the Tampa sports world and I grew up together, UF was the center of the college sports universe during my time on campus.

And it wasn't just Florida's athletes who were achieving their dreams during that timeframe. There were also a number of female sports broadcasters who graduated from UF and were making it to ESPN. Erin Andrews, Laura Rutledge, and Jenn Brown were just a few of the women who carved out their dream paths by working incredibly hard at UF and ultimately making it to the big show. They were achieving their dreams right around the time I was in school or graduating, showing me it was possible to go from the University of Florida to the biggest stage at ESPN in just a few years. Florida has one of the top journalism schools in the country, so it's no surprise the university was producing great talent, and it was clear that ESPN had its eye on Florida for the top stars on the field and in front of the camera.

By the time the Worldwide Leader came to recruit on campus, landing an internship with the network was the hottest ticket in town. ESPN held an information session on campus in the Reitz Union, UF's student union.

As expected, the room was completely packed, and I knew ahead of time that tons of kids would show up with their résumés, which meant that mine would likely end up in a big pile. I wanted to stand out among the group, so I took the name of the ESPN contact off of the pamphlet and emailed him my résumé separately. When everyone else goes left, you go right. I had nothing to lose by putting myself out there, so I took the chance.

It paid off, and I landed an interview with Emanuel Adjekum, who would become one of my guardian angels.

I didn't know this story until many years later, but when I interviewed for the ESPN internship, all fifty spots had been taken. Emanuel believed in me so strongly, he went to numerous people, including high-ranking executives, in order to ensure that I landed an internship spot. That year, I was intern number fifty-one out of fifty. Great things happen when you have the courage to be yourself.

It's also so important to always keep hope alive because you never know when something great is about to happen. That year,

ESPN picked one intern per SEC school, so I was selected as the single representative that summer from the University of Florida. Do not give up on yourself and your dreams, even when the odds are stacked against you, because you never know when you could be intern fifty-one out of fifty. You might be giving up right before the dream is about to become a reality.

Even if a person is tremendously talented, no one can achieve their goals without people opening doors and making their dreams possible. Emanuel will forever be one of those extraordinary, selfless leaders who completely changed my life. Thanks to two other guys, Fred Brown and Joe Franco (Joe started at ESPN the same year the company launched; he's one of the original employees and has a star on the ESPN Walk of Fame), my internship was tailored to make sure I had the best possible experience during my summer at ESPN.

All the interns lived together in a building in downtown Hartford, Connecticut. ESPN helped subsidize the rent. I'm still close with many of the interns today. We get to see each other when we visit each other's cities around the country, and some of those who still work at ESPN have hosted me as a guest on the sets of their TV shows. I was even a bridesmaid in a fellow intern's wedding (Jacquie Berger) ten years after our internship.

The first time I drove to ESPN, I thought I'd gotten off at the wrong exit. I just assumed I'd pull into what felt like Disney World right off the highway. Instead, you exit I-84 onto a pretty rural road, with wide-open green spaces and a few stores and buildings here and there. *Uh, where am I?*

It isn't until you drive a few more miles down what feels like a country road that you finally see ESPN's sprawling campus and satellite dishes. Originally, ESPN (whose initials once stood for Entertainment Sports Programming Network, before officially being changed to just ESPN) chose Bristol because the network needed wide-open areas for their satellite dishes and signals. As we've talked about, internships are a great way to figure out what you do and don't want in a job. In addition to the job responsibilities, you have to test out whether you'd be happy living in that particular area of the country.

ESPN really rolled out the carpet for our internships. Not only did they help with housing, but we were also paid for our internships and taken on some really cool field trips, including to New York City. We had full access to the gym, where sometimes you'd run into the anchors in the locker room, and we got to eat in the famous ESPN cafeteria (affectionately known as the Caf), equipped with an ice cream machine, candy station, entrees of the day, and even an omelet maker, which really came in handy at two a.m. ESPN is also where I became a coffee drinker, as my production hours typically ran from late afternoon until the early hours of the morning in order to cover baseball games.

The first day of the internship, we attended Rookie Camp, otherwise known as ESPN's orientation. From then on, we were assigned a job that every other employee had held at the company. I was a studio production intern, which meant that, at that time of year, I crafted highlights for *SportsCenter* and *Baseball Tonight*. I would be assigned a game to watch, track the plays, and note the highlights I wanted to show on TV. When the game was nearing its end, I'd go into an edit bay with an ESPN editor, and they would cut the plays in the order I envisioned to make a streamlined highlight for viewers to watch. I would then write a shot sheet, which is a general overview and description of the plays, run it across the hall to the anchor hosting the show, and then the host would read my highlight on air. It was an amazing experience. I could call home and say, "The highlight I just created is going to run on ESPN at 11:17 p.m.," so my family would get to watch my work live back in Tampa.

On one of my first days of work, I learned that the system we'd been using as a rundown for the shows was called ENPS. I literally thought they spelled ESPN wrong. (I later learned this is the standard program news stations use across the country for inputting their highlights and keeping track of their show plans.)

Another day when I was in charge of a highlight, the game was fairly standard and low-scoring, and the runs were driven in routinely. But on the other hand, the ball girl had the game of her life, with multiple phenomenal catches. So . . . I made the entire highlight all about the ball girl. I knew that storyline would be much more thrilling to fans, compared to the standard play that drove in the runs.

If you're working in the sports industry, you're probably a sports fan, meaning that you're the best judge of good content. If you find something entertaining or exciting, fans will, too. You have to trust your gut and not be afraid to think outside the box. I remember that highlight being one of my favorites of the entire summer.

As ESPN interns, we were encouraged to share ideas with the company. In fact, we were told that some of the best concepts that the company was still using—and still uses to this day—had been pitched by interns. That was one of the greatest facets of ESPN and a trait I've seen in the best companies—everyone matters and is made to feel like an equal.

One day, it dawned on me that ESPN's Spanish channel should be named "ESPNol," *as in español, but with ESPN's name.* I thought it was genius! So I just went ahead and emailed John Skipper, who was the executive vice president of content at the time and later became the president of all of ESPN. No big deal.

It's truly amazing that John even read my email, with a job as big as his at ESPN. Not only did he read my note, he also wrote me back and told me the company had once considered that option but decided against it. However, in better news, he told me I should come meet with him. He blocked off time on his calendar a few weeks later . . . for me, *an intern.*

I had a wonderful meeting with him. John is one of those rare leaders who truly made me feel like I, and my ideas, really mattered. After genuinely getting to know me, John let me know that the company was planning to launch a women's initiative called espnW. I said, "Perfect! I have on a *W* necklace [because my name is Whitney]. I'm already wearing your gear!"

Everyone had always told me that if I ever wanted to work at ESPN full time, I'd have to start in the middle of nowhere and work my way up for twenty years and then *maybe* I could finally have a shot at ESPN. What that meeting with John helped me realize was that I could carve out my own path—one that may never have existed before. Just because someone hasn't thought of an idea yet doesn't necessarily mean it isn't a good idea. You might just be the one whose intuition and creativity were needed to make that path a reality. After all, *you are the first you.*

I was really sad to leave ESPN at the end of that summer, because I was in the epicenter of my dream job, doing exactly what I wanted to do. It felt like a little bit of a letdown to leave where I was content and happy and return to school. I just kept thinking, *Don't you go to school to get to this point?* But if anything, my summer at ESPN left me surer than ever that working in sports was what I wanted to do.

Upon returning to Gainesville for my senior year, it didn't take much time for me to fall back in love with UF and readjust to school life. I took the internal fire I'd felt at ESPN and channeled it into giving my last year of college everything I had. I reached out to the UF TV station, WUFT, to let them know about my broadcasting experience, my recent tenure at ESPN, and my desire to get involved when I returned to campus. I'm a big believer in being proactive. I don't wait for dreams to fall into my lap. Thanks to the station directors, Mark Leeps and Bridget Grogan, I was given my first shot at on-air reporting as the sports reporter on WUFT's Friday-morning news. The TV station covered North Central Florida, from Gainesville to Jacksonville. Later, someone in an auditorium recognized me as the girl who did sports in the mornings on the station, so I knew I had at least one viewer! It was an incredible opportunity that allowed me to sideline report Gators games and cover Tim Tebow's Pro Day. Reporting from the field in Ben Hill Griffin Stadium, a.k.a. the Swamp, is certainly an experience I will never forget. By the way, one of the coolest and most unique parts of UF is that you can enter the football stadium whether there's a game going on or not; the stadium's gates are open year-round. I still love walking up the ramp to the stadium and seeing the field each time I visit campus. You can't help but get goosebumps.

I also owe a major debt of gratitude to one of my all-time favorite professors, Ted Spiker, who later became the chair of the journalism department. He is one of the main reasons my senior year turned out to be unexpectedly fantastic. Professor Spiker, whom I'm still close with to this day, taught a class called Advanced Magazine Writing. He has the gift of understanding each student's soul, celebrating their passions, and making learning practical and invigorating. We even had a class or two at the famous Swamp Restaurant in Gainesville. (You can't learn on an empty stomach!)

Over a decade later, we still affectionately refer to that class as #WednesdayAfternoons (when the class met), and our class of just a handful of students is still a close group to this day. Ted is the kind of teacher who sets the bar high for all others because he inspires his students to chase their dreams. Motivated by readings in class, I'll never forget Professor Spiker asking each of us what we would do if we each had twenty dollars and could spend it on granting a dream experience. My answer was getting to see the halftime speech in the locker room during a Super Bowl. Out of the thousands of students he's taught, Professor Spiker still remembers that answer.

I've heard so many times that you "just become a number" at a big school. My experience at UF couldn't have been further from that reality. Our class with Professor Spiker had roughly ten to twelve students, an intimate group who became close-knit. Ted not only believed in me wholeheartedly and supported my unique being, but he treated all of us like family. And the feeling was mutual. We got to watch his boys grow up, as well. In my opinion, Professor Spiker is another of those superstar humans who has a high EQ, which stands for emotional quotient, but is referred to as emotional intelligence.In his position of authority, Professor Spiker truly invested in his students. Despite the fact that UF had thousands of students enrolled, I felt a closeness to Professor Spiker and that entire class. Even all these years later, he still supports my passions and dreams.

I think that's why I loved college so much—I picked the University of Florida because I loved all that made it unique, and it loved me right back. Despite its large enrollment numbers, UF truly made me feel like I mattered. I had a personalized experience in the midst of one of the biggest universities in the country. With a dream college experience under my belt, I was ready to hit the real world.

## CHAPTER LESSONS

- Great things happen when you have the courage to be yourself.
- You never know when something great is about to happen.
- None of us can do life alone. You need a tribe of people who will open doors for you.
- Don't be afraid to think outside of the box. You are the best judge.
- Trust your gut. Go for your dreams. You have nothing to lose.
- At the best companies, everyone genuinely matters the same.
- You can carve out a path that may never have existed before.
- Just because someone hasn't thought of an idea yet doesn't necessarily mean it isn't a good idea.
- Be proactive. Don't wait for the perfect opportunity to fall into your lap.

# CHAPTER 4

# POWER PLAYERS

After graduating from college, I experienced the first real transition time in my life. Frankly, up until that point, I'd always known what was coming next. My path had been charted for me. And while friends who were going into the accounting world or going to law or medical school had already known their plan for a year at that point, I graduated without a job lined up.

I had been in talks with espnW about joining their team and was hopeful I'd have the job secured by graduation. However, like any startup, they were taking longer than expected to get off the ground.

That was my first taste of feeling like a disappointment and not being on the path I thought I was "supposed" to follow in order to be considered a success. Everyone else seemed to have their whole life plan ready to go and would be making a smooth transition from college into the real world—*just like you are supposed to do*.

I learned a very important lesson during those days: *patience*. Corporations have a lot of items to attend to on a daily basis. While getting hired may be *your* priority, it's not the number-one item on their list. There are usually multiple departments that have to coordinate during the hiring process. In addition, getting the official signoff to hire a candidate can be a laborious and intricate process. So you have to take some deep breaths and allow the process to work its way through the corporate structure.

And so, in the fall of 2010, I moved back home to Tampa. I had fully expected to carry the high of my college successes right into a dream job. Instead, I was back home in my childhood bedroom, while my peers were off to their first jobs in big cities. It's important to remember that transition times don't define you. They end up being a blip on the radar when you look back on them down the road. You almost forget they even existed, and it typically takes just one job or one person to pull you out of them.

You are also not alone. Everyone—including the most successful people—has gone through rough patches. They are part of life, and it is important during these times that you prioritize self-care. You can't be your best self without having your physical and mental well-being in top shape.

That time at home turned out to be a blessing in disguise. I was able to spend the last few months of Aunt Franci's life with her. She was nearing the end of her battle with ovarian cancer, and I was grateful to be home to be a support system for my family during this horrific time. I remember one occasion when we went to the hospital to visit her after one of her surgeries. She woke up from the anesthesia, and the first thing she asked was, "Did we give Whitney her birthday gift?" That was Franci Rudolph—always thinking of others first. The gift was a necklace with my first initial, which is why, if you see me to this day, I'm most likely wearing a *W* necklace.

I was in contact with espnW during that summer, being reassured the job was on its way. As summer came to a close, my parents were getting weary, as it had been close to five months since I'd graduated and I still didn't have a job. Those time periods in between responsibilities can seem like lifetimes while you are in them. Looking back, you barely remember they existed. When you don't have a routine laid out for you, I'm a big believer in aiming to schedule one activity per day. When you have at least one place to be during the day, you feel a sense of purpose, and the rest of your daily routine often builds upon that first activity and fills itself out. I also tell people that when you're between jobs, you should aim to do one new task every day. The times I've been between roles, I've committed to either applying for a new job each day or reaching out to a new contact. Having that fresh shot every day renews your hope of landing your next opportunity.

During those times when it seems like everyone else around you has it totally figured out, and you feel like you're in a big black hole of the unknown, it's more important than ever to double down on that unwavering belief in yourself. There's a reason you're different, and you have to ask yourself if you'd want to be doing the jobs that those around you are doing—just for the sake of security—or if you really want to give your dream path your best shot. It's also very important during transitions to focus your time on the people and things that bring you joy, and derive hope from the unexpected opportunities or bright spots that may come your way.

My parents finally gave me a deadline. After nearly five months of living at home, unemployed, and with the summer coming to a close, they told me that if this job didn't come to fruition by Labor Day, I was going to have to find another opportunity. I understood, but I was internally very frustrated. I knew from my conversations with the espnW team that a job was looking promising—it was just going to take some time to get to a place where they were ready to hire additional staff. I knew I was meant for this sports path, and the idea of having to give it up went strictly against how my soul was feeling and what I knew was possible. Luckily, with two weeks to go until the Labor Day deadline, I was hired as an independent contractor by espnW. And just like that—literally overnight—I went from unemployed to having a dream job and landing at ESPN right out of college. What a difference a day can make!

My aunt Franci ended up passing away September 18, 2010, so she knew I had secured the job with espnW right before her seven-year battle with ovarian cancer came to an end. I take solace in knowing she was proud that I'd achieved my dream job at the time.

I'm also appreciative that that transition time allowed me to spend the last few months with her. Life has a way of working out for the best. Sometimes, it's just not the way you expect, and you don't always know the "why" at the time.

When someone close to you has a serious illness, it becomes the center of their loved ones' lives. A normal schedule takes a back seat so that all hands can be on deck to help with the loved one's care, so I was grateful that my role with espnW allowed me to work remotely. Talk about everything happening for a reason. I lived at home in Tampa for another year to save money and until our family's lives had returned to a sense of normalcy.

In that first year working for espnW, I was writing, reporting, and editing for W's website, which was espnW's primary content platform, in addition to their social media pages. I had the opportunity to report on amazing stories of personal triumph that covered women's sports and catered to female sports fans. I will never forget reporting on how the One Love Foundation was working to combat domestic violence in honor of Virginia lacrosse player Yeardley Reynolds Love, or how James Shields was changing foster kids' lives by bringing them to Rays games to sit in a suite. Or the forty-nine-year-old college student who had just made the Pepperdine University swim team. I felt like I was on the front lines of the most interesting stories in sports. On top of that, espnW was my first foray into my passion of the intersection of sports and making the world a better place. I often formed close bonds with the families I interviewed, and they became part of my heart. A few months into the job, I was talking about some of the recent stories I'd written, and I clearly remember it hitting me that I had thought I was taking on this job because of my passion for sports and to tell others' stories. In reality, the stories I was writing and the people I was interviewing were changing me for the better.

In addition to the many heartfelt stories I was able to tell and the roundtable I participated in, where I wrote an editorial on my unwavering belief in Tim Tebow, I was also in charge of two daily series: "About Last Night" and "Athlete of the Day." Each day, I'd find a female high school athlete who was doing a great job of leading her sports team. I would then interview her and write a feature article on her. And each night, I'd write the "About Last Night" article, which summarized the biggest events that took place that night in sports for fans to read about the next morning. So I was writing and reporting during the day and doing the same at night. It was the ultimate hustle, but that was in my DNA.

My relentless work ethic paid off, because the harder I worked, the more opportunities I was given. I even got to report live from the red carpet at the Women's Sports Foundation's Annual Salute to Women in Sports, where I came face-to-face with Michelle Kwan, Venus Williams, Laila Ali, Billie Jean King, Abby Wambach, Alex Morgan, and Maya Moore—just to name a few. I also had the opportunity to cover the movie premiere of *Mighty Macs*.

When I accepted the job at espnW, I could never have known the opportunities that would present themselves. I just had faith that I was where I was meant to be and gave the job every ounce of my effort. I think that sometimes we see the results or payoff of a job, but we forget how it all began and what it took to get there. In the beginning, just a few employees were given the keys to this new startup. Success is a lot like an iceberg: we often focus on the 10 percent of glory we're able to see; but likely 90 percent of the process included hard work, dedication, and sacrifice that people never witnessed or knew about.

What was so unique and special about W (besides the fact that we shared an initial) is that I had the opportunity to work for a startup within one of the largest corporations. I loved being able to help build a new entity. I have an uncanny ability to know when a company has great potential way before anyone else has ever heard of it. I was so grateful to work at the largest sports network; but at the same time, we were getting to build our baby. It was really the coolest combination and what my soul desired.

Like with any startup, all the employees had the ability to pitch ideas. As we all know, I'm not exactly shy when I have a burning idea in my gut that I think would be a good fit for an organization. So I pitched an idea to the editorial team about launching a series where we highlighted women who worked on the business side of sports. And thus, Power Players was born.

I began reaching out to high-level female executives in the sports world. The women I contacted were beyond busy, but I will never forget their graciousness in allowing me to interview them. I was able to connect with and write stories on Amy Trask, the first female CEO of an NFL team; Kathy Behrens, the NBA's EVP of social responsibility and player programs; and Sheila Johnson, the vice chairman of Monumental Sports and Entertainment, which owns the Washington Mystics, Wizards, and Capitals. Sheila was the first African American woman to be an owner or partner in three professional sports franchises. Then there was Pam Gardner, the longest-tenured female chief executive in MLB; Kim Williams, COO of the NFL Network; and Sandy Barbour, the athletic director at Cal. Truly, until this series, I didn't realize there were other women like me out there—women who dreamed of a career in sports and were working in big-time front offices. These women were at the highest levels you could reach and still took the time to talk to and trust a twenty-four-year-old just starting out in the industry. They were the definition of leaders because of their character.

In February of 2011, the Friday of Super Bowl weekend, my editor asked me if I could write a story about how much food is consumed at the Super Bowl. Mind you, this was two days before the big game. I had two choices: I could say, *This is impossible, we have no shot.* Or I could make it happen. One thing I will tell you about my soul is that I do not give up until there's not a single solution or pathway left in the universe. So I began reaching out to every single person I could get in contact with at Cowboys Stadium who might be able to provide information for my story. Even though the Super Bowl was being held there in two days, members of the stadium staff wrote me back; and by some miracle, we were able to publish an entire story on Super Bowl XLV, by the numbers. These are some of the facts I learned for that story:

- Four hundred forty-two Jani-King crew members were set to clean the stadium to prepare it for the game.
- After the Lombardi Trophy ceremony, 350 new cleaning-crew members were slated to arrive at midnight and work until 7:30 a.m. to get the stadium back in shape for stadium tours the next morning.
- The crew was set to clean up after a crowd of approximately one hundred thousand, according to the NFL, plus another fifteen thousand party-pass patrons.
- Tons of nachos would be consumed during the game—an estimated twelve tons—including about 144,000 ounces of cheese, or one ounce of cheese for every Green Bay resident.
- Eight thousand pounds of hot dogs would be consumed.
- Eight hundred gallons of ketchup and mustard would be slathered onto hotdogs, burgers, and fries—or about one and a half ounces for every person who can fit into Heinz Field, the home of the Steelers.
- Five thousand pounds of popcorn would be popped.
- Seventy thousand pieces of fresh jumbo shrimp were going to be peeled.
- Fifteen thousand Kobe beef sliders would be grilled.
- Over ten thousand pieces of sushi were going to be prepared.
- Over one hundred thousand pieces of dessert were going to be baked.
- Over ten thousand s'more pops would be made.
- Ten thousand handmade Texas blueberry caramels were expected to be hand-cut and wrapped.
- Two thousand pounds of sugar, one thousand pounds of flour, and one thousand pounds of chocolate were going to be used.
- Fans were set to consume 15,625 gallons of soda. If that were gasoline, it'd be enough to drive your car for three years straight.
- Eight thousand gallons of water, or enough water to make nearly two hundred thousand pounds of Jell-O, would be consumed.
- One hundred sixty tons of ice, which is enough ice to make three hockey rinks, would be dispensed.

Probably didn't know all of that, did you? Me neither. But more importantly, I pulled off a miracle and reported and wrote that entire story the weekend of the Super Bowl, thanks to the amazing team at Cowboys Stadium, who provided all of these facts while getting ready to host the big game.

What truly felt like pulling off an impossible task proved to me that a relentless work ethic and a refusal to give up really can make anything possible. When I started at espnW, I was being paid per article. After this story was published, I was rewarded with a yearly salary. Clearly, hard work does pay off.

After about a year of living and working from home, I decided that while I was very comfortable in my childhood bedroom in my parents' house, I wasn't going to grow much as a person staying there. I needed to take a leap outside of my comfort zone. So I decided to get LASIK eye surgery and move to New York City in the same month. I call it my YOLO month.

In getting LASIK, I went from being legally blind to having 20/15 vision in about a minute and forty-five seconds. My dad often reminds me that when the doctor told me how long the surgery would take, I joked that I didn't have that kind of time—as in two minutes!

Both of those choices changed my life for the better. Sometimes, it just takes putting one foot out there and trusting in your decisions, knowing that the rewards will follow. So the girl who'd lived in Florida her entire life was off to the Big Apple! I knew I wanted to move back to Tampa, but I just wanted a quick adventure beforehand. Prior to leaving, I confidently proclaimed to my family and friends that I was moving to New York City for a year and then I'd be back. Famous last words.

So there I was, in New York City in my first winter ever. A few things that zero people mentioned before I left: (1) Winter is expensive—all the hats, gloves, boots . . . and who the heck has a budget for earmuffs? (2) The sun sets at four p.m. When I later began working at Major League Baseball, work started for me at six p.m. So I'd walk to the subway, basically in the dark, as everyone was coming home from work. It was depressing, and it felt like bedtime when it was only lunchtime. (3) In school, we sing songs about how winter is three months long. That is false. Winter is more like nine or ten months—we'd often still be wearing parkas at MLB Opening Day in April. (4) When you're in your mid-twenties and you experience your first snowstorm, you're likely going to have the same reaction as all the little kids who are also experiencing their first major snowstorm. So during our first blizzard that year, I went tubing down the hill by my apartment, surrounded by kids whose ages were in the single digits. I named my Facebook album from that day "My first blizzard not from Dairy Queen!"

I grew a lot as a person and learned a lot of lessons in that first year in New York, one of which was the implication of being an independent contractor. I'd never been taught the tax rules for different job classifications. When the tax bill came after my first year with espnW, my jaw was on the ground. My tax rate was roughly 20 percent of my entire salary and pretty much all the money I had in my savings account. No doubt, some tears were shed. At the same time, I was advised that some of the salaried writers were being moved to freelancers, so I decided it was best to begin the job hunt once again. So there I was, in the middle of my first real winter ever, with a year lease I'd just signed a few months prior, a broken foot from a stress fracture, and all of my savings were gone. At least I was getting good practice at these transition times!

## CHAPTER LESSONS

- Transition times don't define you. They are exactly that—a transition to greener pastures.
- Even the most successful people go through rough patches.
- During times of unknown, it's essential to prioritize your physical and mental well-being. You can't be your best self without those two components functioning on all cylinders.
- When you're between jobs, have one activity on your calendar each day and take one new action that gets you closer to your next role.
- During transition times, focus on the people and opportunities that bring you joy. Unexpected doors may be opening. Say yes and embrace them.
- Life has a way of working out—sometimes just not the way you expect.
- Success is a lot like an iceberg: we often focus solely on the results, but to get to that point, there was a lot of hard work and sacrifice that others never saw.
- Those who succeed find a way to make impossible tasks possible.
- Sometimes, you have to be the one to take the first leap of faith.
- As an independent contractor, you are responsible for your own taxes. A company does not withhold them for you the same way it would if you were considered a full-time employee.

# CHAPTER 5

# BASEBALL TEST

As I began job hunting, I spent those subsequent few months taking one new action each day to get me closer to my goal of landing my next dream job, whether that was applying for a new role online or reaching out to a contact who might be able to help.

I had multiple rounds of interviews with a major magazine publication, and I walked out of my final interview as confident as ever, completely sure that I'd landed the job.

Spoiler alert: I didn't get the job.

It was an important lesson for me. When that role didn't come to fruition, I felt like the door to a dream job was slammed in my face and that I wasn't going to find anything better. But life worked out for the best. When one door closes, it almost always means a better opportunity is meant to come along.

A few weeks later, I saw an opening on Craigslist for a job at Major League Baseball. I didn't know if it was even real, but I had nothing to lose. So I took a shot and applied for the role.

Turns out the job was *real*.

I reached out to my old friend and mentor, Jonathan Mariner, whom I'd met way back at the 2008 ALCS at Tropicana Field. I let him know about the opportunity, and I have no doubt he put in a good word for me at MLB.com. But I still had to interview and land the job. Reaching out to a contact is a great way of opening the door for yourself, but you have to independently have the skill set and capabilities to secure the job.

It's key *not* to ask a contact if you can have a job at his or her company. I've never heard of an employee being able to *poof!* create a role out of the blue. There are typically lots of layers of approval needed to open up a new position, but what you can do is *offer value* to high-ranking executives at companies. Ask yourself what you can do to improve their lives. Worst-case scenario, you can ask for a few minutes to learn how they got to this point. Most people love being mentors and sharing their own stories. But do not be a time suck. You're much better off figuring out what you can do to improve their roles or add value to their companies. Once you've built a relationship with them, it's much easier to reach out and ask if they can put in a good word for you for an open role. The higher the position, the more pull the individual usually has within their company. But if you just reach out and ask for a job, they are going to shut down. They don't owe you anything, and no relationship has been built.

Back to my interview at MLB.com, otherwise known as MLB Advanced Media. First, I had an introductory interview with HR. A few days after that, I received a call to come back and meet with the leaders of the social media department.

To set the scene, MLB.com is located in Chelsea Market, which is basically a food lover's paradise on the first floor. There are bakeries, artisan food shops, and restaurants galore. I'm also pretty sure it says in a guidebook somewhere to get to Chelsea Market when it opens in the morning and *run*—do not walk—to The Lobster Place, because that's what buses full of tourists do every morning. That made walking in the building for work each day a lot of fun. In the middle of the Market is an elevator with a big MLB.com logo, which would take you up to our offices on the fifth floor. Many Chelsea Market tourists often tried to hop in the elevator, ready to go visit MLB.com's offices, only to learn that, yes, you actually needed a badge to get up there. You couldn't just tour around with your lobster while people were working.

Because food is my best friend, I was obviously blown away when I first arrived at Chelsea Market. I'm an early arriver when I have a commitment. I'd rather be an hour early somewhere than five minutes late. I think it's selfish and inconsiderate to keep people waiting if it can be avoided, though sometimes life happens and people understand. Since I got to Chelsea Market early on this particular day, I shopped around before my interview and stumbled upon some delicious cookies from one of the bakeries that I thought my interviewers might enjoy, as well.

Afterward, when I told my parents, they couldn't believe I'd brought my interviewers cookies, and they were pretty sure at that point that I *definitely wasn't* getting the job. But in my mind, cookies brighten everyone's day, snacks are great at all times, and I'm pretty sure you don't forget the girl who brought you cookies.

And I was right. They *did* love the cookies! And after getting to know each other during the standard interview process, they caught me off guard and told me I'd be taking a baseball test. They exited the room, and I was left alone with the test. *Gulp.*

The test had a bunch of names of players on a piece of paper— maybe around thirty, total—and I was expected to write a paragraph describing each player. Some of them were big names that everyone had heard of. Others were much more obscure names that really hadn't hit the scene yet. For one player, I literally knew *nothing* about him, so I'm pretty sure I wrote, "Sounds Italian"!

I could've completely freaked out in that moment, thrown in the towel, and accepted the fact that I wasn't going to get the job. Instead, I thought, *I may not know some of these lesser-known players, but I will show them what I do know.* So I flipped the paper over, wrote the name of every MLB team, and named at least one player who played on each team.

I got the job.

I've learned that it's important in any interview to focus on what you do know—not what you don't know. If I'd stuck to their parameters of what that test was asking me, I really don't know if I would have landed the role. But I also don't know what they actually wanted to see in that experiment—was it my ability to think outside the box? Or to think on my feet, which is key when you're running social media accounts? I didn't really know; but I did know that my creativity, determination, and knack for thinking on my feet would stand out to them. And that was giving it my best shot.

In a stressful work situation, I advise people to be the flight attendant on the plane who keeps serving drinks. So what does that mean? When you're on a plane and there's turbulence, if the pilot makes an announcement that the flight attendants have to be seated, everyone starts to panic. But no matter the level of turbulence, if the flight attendants keep serving drinks and pushing that cart down the aisle, everyone is put at ease that these bumps are no big deal and that they're going to be fine. So no matter how you feel inside when you're about to give a presentation or step into a big work moment, on the outside always be the flight attendant who keeps serving drinks. If the audience and those around you sense that you are calm, they will feel at ease and trust in you, as well.

When I started the job as social media coordinator at MLB, I had once again landed a dream job. Plus, I was able to get the boot off my broken foot right before the interview, so the timing was perfect.

I started the job in April of 2012, as the season was just kicking off. This job was my first role in social media.

MLB was really one of the first companies to begin using social media as a marketing tool. I often tell kids that if they don't know what they want to do yet, it's okay. My job didn't even exist when I was in high school or college. It hadn't been invented yet.

The key is to find a dream job that resonates with you. I started with the *Monday Night Football* goal. Whatever your dream job is, chase after it relentlessly and be open to the opportunities that come your way throughout your journey. It's important to have the self-awareness to know and accept who you are, what you're meant to do, and who you're meant be with in the world.

In starting my job at MLB, I made the leap from being in content-focused roles to one that was considered marketing for the organization. I point out this distinction because there seems to be a mind-set among companies that roles solely focused on writing or creating content are dispensable (even though they aren't at all, and writers and content creators are extremely valuable and talented). But the minute you move into the marketing department, you are seen as someone who is driving revenue for the organization and helping the bottom line. Those roles are very valuable to companies, so, unintentionally, my shift to a marketing role helped me become less dispensable.

In our roles at MLB.com, we worked from six p.m. until two a.m. However, if a game on the West Coast went into extra innings, it was on us to stay on and continue covering the game. So a lot of times, we ended up leaving between the hours of two and five a.m. I often Googled, "What time does McDonald's start serving breakfast?" because some of those departures from work were more like early mornings than late nights.

But my time at MLB.com was a total ball—no pun intended. I described our office as being like a bar without the alcohol. We had TVs all around the room, we worked late nights, and there were tons of young people. We affectionately called our area the Bullpen, which we shared with the employees who managed the teams' websites. We later moved to our very own highly digitized social media room.

Our job was to cover every baseball game each night from a social media perspective. We had a big spreadsheet with hundreds of cells that we'd basically have memorized by the end of the season. It detailed what each team wanted us at MLB.com to post for them and what the team's social media department would be handling on their own. We worked hand in hand with our contacts at each team. We also had real-time correspondents at every stadium who would send us behind-the-scenes footage to post on the accounts. Some teams wanted us to handle posting the majority of the content, and others preferred just getting some assistance here and there. Essentially, we did everything from posting scoring updates to sharing great fan photos, video highlights, beautiful stadium shots, breaking news, and all the major plays. You really didn't have time to go to the bathroom, because you might miss a major home run!

We also had live-feed access to the games, so there were times we'd share breaking news on the social media platforms before it could even hit the live broadcast.

Each shift, we'd be assigned a couple of games, and we were in charge of making sure everything the club wanted on that spreadsheet was shared on the team's social media channels. As I moved up the ladder, I was also in charge of posting on MLB's official social media accounts. To give you an idea of the timeframe, Instagram came onto the scene while I worked at MLB, so we were posting updates on all different teams at all times and just trying to get the information on each platform as fast as possible. Our group was also in charge of writing posts on our blog, Cut4, as well as aggregating tweets covering major events on our 140 Club, which was our Twitter hub.

We worked pretty much every night, weekend, and holiday. I started as the third or fourth person in our ballpark department, and it grew to about twenty people during my time there. We were all young and truly like a big family, so I didn't mind spending all of those hours together. We made sure to have a blast, and we often saw our coworkers more than our loved ones.

We were frequently asked what we'd do during the off-season. My answer was always, "When is that?" Our jobs were truly 24/7. Instead of working until two a.m., our shifts ran until midnight during the "off-season." By the time the World Series festivities ended in late fall, we'd go right into roster moves and personnel changes, followed quickly by Winter Meetings. All of a sudden, it was February, pitchers and catchers were reporting, and a new season was upon us, with Spring Training right around the corner.

Hurricane Sandy struck during the 2012 season. Even though I'd lived in Florida my whole life, I'd never encountered a direct hit by a hurricane. Then I move to New York City and suddenly I get hit by a hurricane? It was crazy. Power was out for a long time up to about 40th Street in Manhattan. Luckily, I lived on 42nd Street, so I was one of the few people in my entire department who had power. Unfortunately, I also happened to have mono. So I was basically running all the team accounts from my apartment while, at the same time, trying to keep my eyes open and get through mono. It certainly was a wild time.

I will never forget that when I started at MLB.com, I was really the first woman in the department who mainly worked nights. The first week, I took the subway home, but that was terrifying at four a.m. Finally, I got up the nerve to approach my boss. To my department's credit, they began reimbursing employees for their cabs home if they left late at night, because I spoke up. Above all the work stuff I've ever accomplished, getting that cab rule passed has always stuck with me because I felt like I was looking out for the safety of all the future employees. While in my first week, I was scared to make such a big ask, I ultimately realized it was a safety issue *and* a human one. I wasn't being overly demanding or entitled; it was about employee well-being. That was a big lesson for me—safety is *always* first. So if you're ever worried about your security, absolutely speak up. Your employer likely wants to do everything possible to help you.

Another of my major contributions to the department was the Social Concession Stand, affectionately known as @SocialConcess on Twitter. As we've established, food is my best friend. I thought, *How can we have baseball going on around the clock with no concession stand?* (Also, to be fair, Chelsea Market and many of the surrounding restaurants were closed when we'd get hungry in the late hours of the night.) So being the innovator I am, I thought, *I must fix this immediately.* And thus, Social Concess was born. Everyone was in charge of bringing in candy to contribute, and then whenever we were hungry, we could grab a snack. When employees would go on vacation or to the grocery store, it warmed my heart to see that Social Concess was usually front of mind, as they'd often return to work with a bag full of snacks to contribute.

Another of my favorite parts of the job was becoming so close with a lot of the social media managers at the teams. Since we worked hand in hand, we spoke on a daily basis and truly became like family. One of those amazing human beings was Michael Harris, who ran marketing for the Philadelphia Phillies. Later down the road, as he was working to build out the team's social media staff, he brought me down to interview for one of the openings in the department. I sat at the press-conference table and kiss the grass on the field—it was a dream day. Michael and I still keep in touch.

Naturally, there were many highs and lows throughout those two years, and I made mistakes. Social media is a live microphone, and there were times I tweeted the wrong scores or updates. I quickly deleted and fixed, but I'm forever appreciative of the bosses and team contacts who forgave me, saw them as a learning experience, and ultimately realized that I brought more good than bad to the table. But in any social media role, even if you delete the post, you have to remember that people have likely already seen it or taken a screenshot—especially if you're running a corporate account. Because I had perspective on the fleetingness of life at such an early age, I always felt that if no one was dying, the mistake wasn't that big a deal. In my mind, if it could be deleted and immediately corrected, that was a pretty good solution, as far as mistakes go. But obviously, the teams are huge brands, and errors were a big deal to everyone—understandably so. Being a perfectionist, I used to dwell on the mistakes I made, and they would eat me up inside. I learned that it's so important to be accountable and accept responsibility and then correct the issue as quickly as you can. But from then on, you have to focus on what you can control and move forward. It was really in that job that I accepted the fact that I am human, I'm going to make mistakes, and dwelling on them isn't going to do me any good. It was at MLB.com that I could feel myself improve and grow as a person into someone who was better able to move on from her mistakes. I always learned from them, but I also did my best to not let them eat me alive for days afterward.

However, I always challenge people to make sure there is an obvious upside in their posts. If there's not much gain from a social media post, but there could be a massive downside, *do not post*. It's just not worth it.

One gut-reaction post I'll never forget and that became a highlight of my time at MLB.com took place during the 2013 Super Bowl in New Orleans. *What is it with me and epic Super Bowl moments?*

Typically, we had a small staff on days like the Super Bowl because all people talk about on that day is football, football, and *maybe* the commercials. Baseball usually isn't front of mind. So I was the only lead person on that evening, and in charge of (wo)manning the MLB social media channels.

Suddenly, in the third quarter of the game, the lights went out. Everyone was looking around, wondering what to do; but almost instantly, when people realized it was a technical issue and that they weren't in danger, everyone turned to their phones to react to the wild situation. This was at a time before brands really jumped into world events. If you remember, brands even *having* social media accounts was still new at this time. So when the lights went out, I thought it'd be savvy for baseball to jump in and say hello to the world. So I quickly wrote out a tweet and sent it to my boss for approval, and off it went. It just said, "We thought we'd take this brief pause to remind you that pitchers and catchers report in 8 days." The tweet went viral. It was the same year that Oreo put out their famous tweet during the blackout, so both of them really caught people's attention, and our brands found a way to win the moment. Our tweet in no way brought down the NFL; it just took advantage of the downtime to unexpectedly promote MLB when people least expected it. *When everyone else goes left, you go right*. The tweet garnered over seven thousand retweets, got a ton of media press, and earned me a personal thank-you from the CEO of MLB.com. Shortly thereafter, I was given a full-time position, after working the first year or so as a part-time employee.

It was an epic moment that neither I nor the company will ever forget. I felt in my gut that the idea would be a success, and I went for it.

About two years into my time at MLB.com, I felt a nag in my gut that said I was missing too many events in my personal life—too many Mother's and Father's Days, too many holidays, too many friends' weddings. I knew these activities weren't going to happen again. It's really important to audit how every experience makes you feel. MLB Advanced Media did all they could to give employees time off for important personal occasions; but at the end of the day, it's a sport that happens while almost everyone else is off from work, so you're working while your loved ones are enjoying off time together.

As you take on new jobs and are put in different situations, your priorities and what your heart really needs become clearer over time. Listen to your heart. For me, missing out on those personal experiences and memories, especially after losing so many close relatives early on, made me realize that compromising those happy moments was not negotiable for me. You can't take or stay in a job for superficial reasons or to make anyone else happy. All people care about in your life is that you are happy and good to them.

In life, you don't have to have chapters 4, 5 and 6 figured out. You just need to figure out what the next best step is for you. I realized that I likely wasn't going to go from night shifts at MLB.com to CEO of the company any time soon. And like most sports, baseball is seasonal, so more people are needed during the months when the games are played. I was lucky enough to stay on year-round; but a lot of times, sports organizations trim down their staffs in the off-season, as we did ours. Employers, as a whole, are going to do what's best for them; so, by that same token, you have to do what's best for you as an employee. In fact, in any relationship dynamic—whether it's work, personal, or friendship—if you're not 100 percent happy, it means there's something else better out there for you.

*You are the first you*, so you have to be the one to go and chase exactly what your heart needs. I knew my heart needed a shift in priorities.

## Chapter Lessons

- When an opportunity doesn't come to fruition, know that an even better one is meant to come along.
- A contact can open the door for you to interview for a position, but you have to do the work from there to land the job yourself.
- You can ask a contact at a company to pass along your résumé or put in a good word for you for an open position, but the vast majority of the time, an employee can't just create a job opening for you at their company.
- Take the time to build relationships with executives. If you reach out and ask for a job, they're most likely going to shut down or ignore you. But if you take the time to provide them value or build a relationship *first*, when the time comes, they'll be much more willing to recommend you for an open position.
- If you don't know the answers to what they're asking in an interview, show them what you *do* know. Don't be afraid to step outside the box and be creative.
- Always be the flight attendant who keeps serving drinks.
- If you don't know what you want to do now, it's okay. My job at MLB didn't even exist when I was in college.
- When you're in a role that generates revenue for a company, you will be seen as more valuable to management.
- Identify a dream job, chase after it relentlessly, and be open to the opportunities that come your way that may be an even better fit for you.
- Speak up if you ever feel your safety is in question. Your employer will absolutely understand. You're not acting entitled when your well-being is at stake.
- Social media is a live microphone. You have to make sure there are clear pros to your post and not much downside or risk.

- Every job you take is going to further clarify your priorities. Listen to what your heart needs the most at the time.
- You can't take a job for superficial reasons or to make anyone else happy. The goal is to make sure your heart is happy. Those around you just care that you are good to them, and they will admire your authenticity.
- You don't need to have chapters 4, 5, and 6 figured out in life. You just have to figure out the next best step for you.
- Employers are going to do what's best for them, so you have to do what's best for you.
- If you're not 100 percent happy in any relationship dynamic, it means there's something better out there for you.

# CHAPTER 6

# Pizza to the Gate

In November of 2013, I was sitting at LaGuardia Airport, waiting to catch a flight for a quick trip home to Tampa. At each gate in the Delta terminal, there are tables with their own individual iPads, where you can search different news outlets, track flight times, play games, and—most importantly for me—order food to the gate.

My favorite restaurant in all of LaGuardia is a pizza place called Crust, located in Terminal D. While I was sitting at the gate and scrolling through the iPad, I realized I could order a pizza right to the gate from Crust. Like, they would *walk it over to me*. Life. Made.

While I was eating (an entire pizza by myself), I decided to peruse the iPad for some entertainment. I pulled up the *New York Times* app (I'm a news junkie and love to read), and the first story I came across was about a company called VaynerMedia.

It was the first company I'd ever read about that was doing social media for a variety of different companies at once, a.k.a. a social media agency. In addition, I could tell that VaynerMedia was run like a family and that it was a company where culture was prioritized. I instantly knew it was where I belonged. Jobs are often like spouses: you can't always picture the right fit—you just know it when you see it.

So I got on the plane, bought Wi-Fi, figured out this guy Gary Vaynerchuk's email address, and wrote him a note that said something along the lines of, *I just read about you at Gate D4, and I need to come work for you.* I think I attached my résumé, as well.

Being at that gate that day and reading that story was one of the most fateful and luckiest moments of my life, not to mention that Gary even read my email in the first place. He then forwarded it to his HR department, and an interview was arranged. Fun fact: Most companies have the same email format for all of their employees, so if you can find one email address (a PR, media, executive, or HR contact at the company), you can probably figure out the email address of the contact you're trying to reach.

The best decision you can ever make in your entire job search is to find a boss who sees the world the same way you do. You can land your dream job, but if your boss doesn't believe in you and allow you to be yourself, it's not going to work out long-term (similar to a spouse). On the flip side, a boss who truly believes in you will open many doors and opportunities for you—even if the job started out not being your dream position. People will forever sell what they believe in, and if you make an impact on someone, you're going to be front of mind for them when opportunities arise.

Like any relationship dynamic—similar to romantic relationships and friendships—find a boss who thinks you hung the moon, and vice versa.

I had my first interview with Vayner a month later, in December of 2013. The first round was a really cool format. I met with a number of employees at the company to make sure that I would be a culture fit. I felt 100 percent comfortable being myself, which is a feeling I now look for as an indicator of a right fit for any venture or partnership I enter.

In January of 2014, after the holiday festivities had settled down, I was invited back for a second interview. I met with some additional employees and remember liking everyone. This round, I also met with one of the more adult executives, who assessed my capabilities for the role.

Throughout the entire interview process, I was being considered for an account executive position. I was told that Vayner had a rolling interview process, in which they'd vet candidates who seemed to be a potential fit at the company; and then the moment a position became available, they already had the identified candidate in the pipeline. So while the second interview also went well, I left thinking that maybe I'd hear from them in six months, or whenever a position opened up.

I received a note the next day offering me a job, and it was for an even higher position than I'd interviewed for—a senior account executive.

It's so important to go where and to whom you are wanted. It's a waste of time and energy to try to convince a person or company to love you when there are people out there who already do. Save yourself some energy and headaches by embracing those who embrace you. Before I ever stepped through the door for my first day of work, Vayner had already tripped over themselves to show me—when they didn't have to—how much they valued and wanted me. You can learn a lot about a company by how they treat you during the interview process.

When I showed up for my first day of work, I called my parents and told them I'd found an island of my people. Everyone was kind, outgoing, and friendly. I often say that working at VaynerMedia validated my whole life because it was the first place where I learned about EQ, or emotional intelligence. Not only had no one ever given my skill set a name, but I'd never been in a place that prioritized people with high EQs above all other personality traits. Gary said that he felt those with high emotional intelligence perform better in business because they can read people and situations really well. Emotional intelligence essentially refers to your ability to interact with and understand people. I'd never even heard the term before—turns out it was my superpower all along!

Gary was the greatest teacher I've ever had, and the only boss who made it seem like I was the employee he'd been waiting for.

When I'm around a person, I can almost instantly tell you the kind of person they are, their confidence level, and why they act the way they do. It almost feels like X-ray vision into a person's soul. I'm constantly told that I should be a therapist because I can sum people up and, therefore, give them the guidance they need to improve their lives. So it makes sense that I ended up in marketing. If I can help people become the best versions of themselves, I certainly can do the same for brands.

I started working on some of the major brands at Vayner, which, because of their large-scale nature, were much slower moving and more corporate. On my third day at Vayner, the owner of the Miami Dolphins invested in the company, and he and Gary paired together to create a fund that would invest in startups. Major credit to Gary, who plucked me out of my original role and created an entirely new job for me—one that was the perfect fit for my skill set and personality. Once an investment was made in those companies and they needed marketing help, they'd be handed over to me, and I was able to use my creativity and vision to help the newly formed companies flourish.

One of the many aspects I loved about Vayner was that an imperfect fit was not anyone's fault. For example, if a manager and an employee didn't get along, one of the two wasn't necessarily held responsible. Often, a switch was made so the employee and manager could be paired with different people. The same went for employees and their clients. Gary handpicked the absolute perfect soulmate of a role for my skill set and personality. It wasn't that the first position was negative in any way; he just found the perfect match for me. And that was one of the many aspects that made the company a fit for me. Personnel- and brandwise, it was all about chemistry and finding your perfect match.

I also loved that Vayner was well established and had top-tier clients, but it functioned like a startup. You didn't necessarily have to follow the standard process of climbing the corporate ladder. I didn't have to be a coordinator before I was a manager before I was a vice president, etc. On any given day, the company assessed what jobs were needed and who could get them done. I loved that I could be plucked off of one role (by the CEO!) and have a new one created just for me by Gary himself. Deep down, I have always been ready to make important decisions, and I can typically read exactly what a dynamic needs to improve. Vayner was the first place that didn't make me wait until I was in my sixties to hold a high-level executive position or to make it to the top rung of the corporate ladder. Here I was, at twenty-six years old, employee number 167 (as I was told), making executive decisions for entire companies in which people had invested substantial money.

The autonomy of my new role was what I'd craved my whole life: someone who empowered me to trust my gut and to make the decisions I knew were best. Gary and the other executives were always there if I had a question, but they let me completely fly in the decision-making process. Gary knew that even if we made our worst mistake, we weren't going to blow up the company. The trust happened in the hiring process; and once you were part of the team, you were empowered, supported, and not micromanaged, because—let's be honest—it's the worst when a boss does that. I finally had full autonomy in a role, which was the first time my soul felt content in a job.

By using creativity and strategic partnerships, I was able to help grow and market the Vayner RSE companies that became my clients. Because of my success in helping to grow those brands, Gary and his team began giving me the sports clients at Vayner, which included the Miami Dolphins.

I had the opportunity to work hand in hand with the Dolphins' marketing and social media teams to enact the latest technologies and strategies in order to help grow the brand. We worked on such innovative campaigns that our work was nominated for awards, and we helped sell season tickets in the new stadium. Additionally, using the latest social media capabilities, we also optimized partnerships with sponsors, so both the sponsor and team saw the best results of their partnership, and both brands benefitted from the new tactics. One of the awards for which we were nominated was a direct-response campaign in which we came in second to Justin Bieber. Probably the greatest accomplishment of my lifetime.

All of a sudden, I had gone from a job at MLB.com where I was low on the totem pole, helping to execute the strategies *that others had set in place* for sports teams, to taking a leap of faith—seemingly jumping completely outside of sports—to work at VaynerMedia, where I was now the one in the driver's seat, making the calls for a major professional sports team. That's what happens when you find people who believe in you. In the decision to join VaynerMedia, I had trusted my instincts and, for the first time, made the decision that 100 percent filled up my heart. As we've talked about, you cannot take any job for superficial reasons or to make anyone else happy. All the people in your life care about is that you are happy and good to them.

I learned one of my greatest life lessons in that role, as well. When I was given the Dolphins as a client, I realized that one of my main contacts at the team was the brother of a girl who had lived in my dorm during my freshman year at the University of Florida. Had I not been nice to her, he could have easily conveyed my poor reputation to my bosses at Vayner, and I could've lost my biggest career opportunity thus far. Luckily, she and I were friends, but it's just so important to take the high road (a big Gary V. lesson) because you never know when a person is going to come back into your life and you're going to need them.

Our initial three-month contract working with the Dolphins went really well, and then we had an opportunity to present a longer-term strategy in order to continue working together. Three of us were scheduled to fly down to Miami to present our yearlong strategy to many high-ranking members of the Dolphins organization. While our VP on the account, Mickey Cloud, had caught a slightly earlier flight that evening, my coworker, Nik Bando, and I were stuck on the tarmac at LaGuardia, with no sign of takeoff in sight. American Airlines continued to delay our flight and finally brought us back to the gate around eleven p.m. (The flight attendants had hit their max working hours after all the delays.) And, of course, they canceled the flight. The rescheduled flight the next morning wouldn't get us in until well after the presentation had begun. So, while all the passengers waited in line, I got on the phone with American Airlines and discovered there was a flight at the crack of dawn—around six a.m.—that was leaving JFK. The airline agent told me they had one seat left. I'm not one to take no for an answer, so I remained on the line and spoke to the customer service representative until I was able to persuade them to miraculously come up with a second seat for Nik. #NoVaynerEmployeeLeftBehind

After waiting in line for about another hour for our car and hotel vouchers, Nik and I took a car service to a Holiday Inn in Jamaica, Queens; I showered; I slept for maybe an hour; and then we were on our way to JFK Airport at around four a.m. When we got to the gate (thank goodness the plane was on time), American Airlines let me know they were running out of overhead space, and I was going to have to check my bag. But if I waited for it at baggage claim in Miami, we were going to be late to the presentation. After all we'd been through, I couldn't let a checked bag be the cause of my demise. So I struck a deal with the gate agent that I would risk taking my bag on the plane to find overhead space, and if there didn't end up being any, my bag would have to be checked on the next flight. *Who even cared about clothes at this point?* I walked onto the plane; and, sure enough, there was plenty of overhead space. I put my bag up, and we took off on time. We landed in Miami about an hour before the presentation, quickly grabbed a ride over to Hard Rock Stadium, and there was Mickey, standing in the parking lot to greet us with warm Chick-fil-A breakfast sandwiches for Nik and me. I've never seen a more beautiful sight in my life. Mickey delivered what we needed most at the moment: comfort, familiarity, and food. We gave the presentation as a team, it went great, and we earned the longer contract.

It's stories such as these that really put a smile on my face about Vayner. It was all about hustle, and you could earn all you'd ever dreamed of if you worked for it. I am the type of person who is totally fine being accountable for my actions, but I cannot live with not getting to execute my ideas. I have no problem trying and failing, but I can't have the ideas stuck in my soul. I fully accept responsibility, but more often than not, when I have a burning idea and I'm able to execute it the way Vayner allowed me to, magic happens. It was the first place that really affirmed I was an entrepreneur.

And more than anything, Vayner was a big family. Of any place I've ever worked, my biggest group of friends is still from that company. When anything good or bad happens, they are the first people there for me. I'd finally met my people—my soulmates. And they truly loved me in return.

I was finally happy culturally and felt like I was exactly where I belonged. I even remember thinking at one point, similar to how people assess a marriage, *Wow, I could really see myself being here my entire life*—which was also Gary's dream. He joked that he wanted everyone to die still working for him, and he'd just keep creating roles for every employee until they all had their dream jobs. To him, his company was a family; and once you were part of it, he wanted you in the mix forever. And that's the best way to summarize the company as a whole—it was run with the same love and respect you'd show your own family.

One of my other moments of total fate at Vayner was the moment Tim Tebow walked in the door. Not only did we go to Florida at the same time (and won championships together, as we've established), I've always loved Tim as a person and admired his character. He's up there with Oprah for me. He ended up having a meeting at VaynerMedia, and I think I stopped breathing the minute he walked in the door. I'd worked at all these major sports companies, and I never in a million years thought that moving to a small agency would lead to Tebow coming into the office. It was another *best day* of my life. And more than anything, I learned the lesson that when you truly follow your heart, that's when all your dreams really come true.

Every job helps clarify your priorities. For me, working more standard daytime hours so that I could spend my off time with family and friends, along with a healthy culture, became essential to me as I made the move to Vayner. At each stage of your life, it's so important to assess what your priorities are at that moment and how they've changed over time.

The best decisions in life are made when you're so excited about the pros that you don't even think about the cons. That's the feeling I had when I first read the article about Vayner. It was simply where I belonged and what was meant for my life.

Gary made it the number-one rule that all the employees had to get along and treat each other like family. That goes back to the hiring process of selecting employees with high EQs. Gary's thinking was that if people didn't get along, they weren't going to work well in business. But a company full of people who like each other? That's when magic and efficiency happen.

Vayner's culture prioritized authenticity, which is the quality people find most attractive in other human beings. The more unique and true to yourself you were, the more celebrated you were at the company. This approach truly fostered self-confidence, and the employees learned to be more authentic to who they were as people. On top of that, the more real someone was, the more we were taught to respect that person at the company, a directive that came from the top. So we had an entire office of people who were comfortable and celebrated for being exactly who they were. I'd never been in a building where I felt like I could be more me, and that leadership approach is truly the key to anti-bullying and eliminating cliques.

The company was run like a family and based on common sense. All the standard rules at most companies where they do things because that's what they think they should be doing or that's how it's always been done were eliminated at Vayner. It was so refreshing. For example, we weren't stuck with ten or fifteen vacation days a year. As long as we got our work done, we could do what we needed to do in our free time, for our souls. We had "All Hands" meetings, where Gary would give us the latest updates on the company and the most up-to-date insights we needed to know to do our jobs well. There was no standard corporate structure where you had to be in one position before you were promoted to the next role. We also constantly had companies come in to tell us about their newest capabilities, so we were on the forefront of the latest technologies. I felt like I was constantly learning.

Above all else, the advice I learned from Gary completely changed my life, and it's helped me both personally and professionally. He is the greatest teacher I've ever had. (He was my next Oprah.) Here are a few Gary V. lessons that I use as north stars:

- Ninety-nine percent of things don't matter. What's bothering you now will likely be forgotten in a week or even by tomorrow. Unless it's about health or family, it's not really a big deal. Smile through it and let it go.
- Always take the high road. You never know when someone is going to come back into your life and you will need them.
- Gary wrote a book called *Jab, Jab, Jab, Right Hook: How to Tell Your Story in a Noisy Social World*. It basically translates to Give, Give, Give, Ask. Always provide value first in any relationship dynamic. This also applied when we posted content on behalf of brands. If you ask consumers to take an action right off the bat, they're going to scroll over your post. But if you first provide value to them and build a relationship, when you come around with the ask, it's the least they can do to support you in return. The same goes for any personal or business relationship in your life. Always think about how you can provide value first, so you can build a genuine relationship and when you need something, the person will be there for you in return. Don't make an *ask* to benefit yourself. The way to bring value is to reverse engineer and figure out what really enhances a person's or brand's life.
- Self-awareness is the most important trait. Have the confidence to accept exactly who you are, what you're good at, and what you are meant to do in this world. Once you've recognized exactly who you are, go all in on your strengths. Double, triple,

go a thousand times down on what you're good at. Outsource your weaknesses. In the business world, no one cares if you're well-rounded. They want you to have a niche and be the expert at it. If you give your all to improving your weaknesses, you'll only get a little better and be middle-of-the-road at best. But if you focus on your natural gifts and spend all of your time honing those skills, that's how you're going to change the world and carve out a path *to be the first you.*

- People can always tell your intent. Don't try to trick them. Those around you can tell what you're trying to accomplish and if your intent is to get something from them. Be authentic and pure in all of your relationships.

- Depth over width. It's much more valuable to go all in on a few people and have them become your champions for life than to lightly touch a thousand people at once. You're just not going to make as much of an impact attempting to reach the masses as you are going all in and building real relationships with a few people. Once people fully believe in you, they will sell you to everyone around them for life.

- Don't get too high on the highs or low on the lows. Do your best to be as even-keeled as possible, because when things are good, they're going to get worse; and when they're bad, they're going to get better. Life is just easier if you don't put yourself on a constant emotional roller coaster.

- Marketers ruin everything. If you're the first to showcase your product or business in a particular way, consumers are going to be blown away by your creativity. But once other marketers figure out your tactic, they're going to infiltrate a product and inundate consumers with ads. That drives people away from using that product. As an example, when we see banner ads online or a billboard, we often gloss right over them because we know a company is marketing to us.

- Access is the best form of content. Document, don't create. So many people are focused on building a brand and concocting a whole performance about their lives, when all people want to see is the authentic behind-the-scenes of other people's lives.
- Market in the day, month, and year we live in. And market where people's eyes are. Consumers aren't going to come find you. You have to go to where they are. Once people start migrating to a new app or location, find a way to market there before everyone else does, which leads me to my last major takeaway:
- Be a first-mover. If you're the thousandth person to do something, people don't really care. If you're the first, you're going to get all the attention. In essence, *be the first you.*

After about a year and a half at Vayner, the company had grown rapidly. We now had hundreds of employees. Gary had become incredibly famous and was writing books and speaking all over the world, so he was focusing on his personal brand. When I started working at VaynerMedia, the company was made up of mostly college-aged individuals. (I was there when we had to create a nursing room because one of our employees was pregnant.) With all the growth, the company was evolving into a more standard model with formal processes, which is necessary when you are adding hundreds of employees. I'd gone there to work for Gary as my boss and in a startup environment. I'd also been in New York for four years at that point (remember how I was only going to live in New York City for a year?), and my lease was up and my landlords were raising the rent. Right around that same time, I got a call from a startup in Tampa offering me a job.

## Chapter Lessons

- You can order a pizza right to the gate at LaGuardia.
- Jobs are often like spouses—you can't predict the person or opportunity that will present itself; you just know it's the right fit when you see it. Have the self-awareness to know who you are so that you know when the perfect fit walks in the door.
- If you can figure out one email address format at a company, you can probably figure out the address of the person you're looking to reach.
- Find a boss who sees the world the same way you do.
- Embrace dynamics that allow you to be 100 percent yourself. Those are the best fits for your life and happiness.
- It's so important to go where and to whom you are wanted. Don't waste energy trying to convince people to like you.
- If an employee and manager aren't a fit or a client isn't the perfect fit for an employee, it might not be one person's fault. Likely, it's just about the chemistry, and there's a better match out there for both parties that will allow them to flourish.
- The greatest success comes from decisions that fill up your heart 100 percent.
- The best decisions are made when you're so excited about the pros that you don't even think about the cons.
- Your priorities are going to be further clarified after every job. Listen to what your heart needs most at every stage of life.
- Authenticity is the most attractive quality in a person.
- Some of the greatest lessons I learned from Gary V.:
    - Always take the high road. You never know when you're going to encounter that person again.
    - Jab, Jab, Jab, Right Hook. Give, Give, Give, Ask. Always provide value first to those in your life in order to build

a relationship.

- Self-awareness (and accepting exactly who you are) is the most important trait you can possess.
- Depth over width. It's much more valuable to build real relationships with a few people than it is to scratch the surface with the masses.
- Go all in on your strengths.
- Don't get too high on the highs or low on the lows. Do your best to stay zen for as much of life as possible.
- People can always tell your intent. Always be your authentic self in your relationship dynamics.
- Market in the day, month, and year we live in.
- Marketers ruin everything.
- Market where people's eyes are.
- Be a first-mover. That's how you'll change the world.

# CHAPTER 7

# SNOWBIRD FOR THE WINTER

*You can take the girl out of Tampa, but you can never take Tampa out of the girl.* If no one famous ever said that quote, they absolutely should have.

During the time I was at VaynerMedia, it was no secret that my heart was always in Tampa. My desk was adorned with family photos and Tampa sports memorabilia. In fact, during my first week at the company, someone mentioned that VaynerMedia's chief financial officer (CFO), Scott Heydt, lived in Tampa. He tells the story of how I came right into his office, plopped myself on his couch, made myself comfortable, and said, "I hear you live in Tampa!"

Scott commuted back and forth from Tampa to New York City during the majority of my time at Vayner. His growing family was based in Tampa, so he'd travel to Vayner's offices in Manhattan during the week. Scott and I had many fun run-ins at both airports, and the two of us had the Tampa-to-New-York-City flight routes down pat and could easily rattle off which airlines were flying to and from each destination and what times they took off. I also saw Scott many times at the airport at the crack of dawn, and you'd better love your coworkers like family (which we did) to have run-ins at that hour. Scott also flew from New York City to Tampa at least once with my mom and me, so it was truly one big happy family at the end of the day. But Scott shared a connection to Tampa with me during my time away from home, which was a link for me to my family and the city I love, and I look back fondly on that special bond.

So when I got a call from a mobile startup company offering me a job back in Tampa, it felt like a shooting star. I was also dating someone who worked for the Tampa Bay Lightning (he obviously lived in Tampa), so there were a number of factors pulling me back home. When I'd left four years earlier, Tampa's main sports properties were its three pro teams. I couldn't imagine at the time that Tampa would later become home to an abundance of startups and sports organizations, as well as home to many pro athletes.

As my years in New York City passed by and my career path evolved, I often wondered, *What is it that could possibly bring me back to Tampa?* I literally thought my only choice was to work at a sports team. I'd arrived in New York writing for espnW. But in my four years in the city, I'd evolved to doing social media for MLB; and now I was at a startup (Vayner), working for an entrepreneur, with sports entities, at a company whose slogan was, "Marketing in the Year We Live In." I thought, *How the heck am I going to be able to move home without sacrificing all that I've built in my career?*

So when the call came in from the mobile startup offering me a job, I thought this was it. If I turned it down, I had no idea when such a forward-thinking opportunity would come around again. And who knew how long I'd be stuck in New York City by that point?

Also, moving apartments in Manhattan is a nightmare. And the idea of not having to do that, since my lease was up, sounded great to me. In addition, I have always been a grinder and put my career first. I was dating my first boyfriend at this point, and I wanted to prioritize my personal life for once and give love a shot. We both lived in different cities, so eventually, one of us was going to have to make a sacrifice and move to give the relationship its best chance of succeeding.

I knew New York City wasn't long-term for me, and no matter what happened with my relationship, I was going to be moving back home. Additionally, the question of *What if?* is my worst nightmare. I'd always rather give any opportunity my best attempt, and if it doesn't work out—well, so be it. I'd rather try and fail than have to wonder what could've happened if I'd really gone for it. I *always* go for it. I know I will have experiences and learn lessons that help me grow as a person, no matter the outcome. Life is often about the journey, and that's usually where we grow the most. With both the job and the boy, I was leaving it all on the field.

As Vayner was growing and evolving, I had to accept that my dream job wasn't being the VP on a brand's advertising account. I loved Vayner and my fellow employees, so it was really hard to say goodbye. That said, I also realized that I couldn't stay in a city just for the people—especially in a transient city like New York, where many friends would be moving on, as well. When someone is meant to be in your life, you'll keep in touch and find ways to see each other, no matter the distance. On my end, I knew I was once again listening to my heart and focusing on the most important priorities at the time. So in September of 2015, I was homebound back to Tampa.

As an added bonus, I was also able to negotiate my same New York salary in Tampa, which was my first wakeup call to the difference living in an income-tax-free state can make in your life. I couldn't believe the significant bump in my paychecks, simply because I was living in Florida, which is a state that doesn't have income tax. I learned as my career went on that athletes really love playing games in Florida because there's no income tax taken out of those game checks. When you're making millions (or any amount, for that matter), that extra money can make a huge difference in your salary and in your life.

In the four years I lived in New York City, I was able to double my salary. I look back on those early days and still don't know how I made it in the Big Apple on my initial salary—especially when about half of my paycheck went to taxes before I ever saw a penny of it. But I also held three jobs in my four years in the city, and each time I made a job move, I had the leverage to negotiate a higher salary. I would often tell myself, *I'm happy where I am, so I'm not going to make the next job leap unless I'm incentivized.* I was also promoted within the majority of those jobs, so that helped bump me up, as well. However, my biggest increases came from moving jobs. I believe that *the start* of a job is the best time to negotiate. Once you sign your contract, you don't have nearly as much leverage because you're already working for the company, so let a company know all your non-negotiables up front.

I admire people who stay at companies for eighteen years and have that kind of loyalty. But I strongly believe the best way to increase your salary is to move around regularly, because you can negotiate a bump each time you take a new job. However, if you move every two seconds, that's a red flag. If you can, it's a good idea to stay at each job for at least a year. But as long as you have a story and valid reasons for why you moved, interviewers typically understand your timeframes and jumps.

For the most part, once you work at a company, they kind of take you for granted. It's not that they don't greatly appreciate your work; they just complacently view you as an employee who's part of the team, and you aren't front of mind or the most pressing priority. It's kind of like dating. When you stop courting a person and no longer prioritize them, they're going to bolt. Always make those you care about feel like they are number one in your life. Don't take anyone for granted, or you could risk losing them. And both in companies and in relationships, it's often too late to start treating people like a million bucks once they have one foot out the door. They need to be prioritized and celebrated the whole time they are in your presence.

When you live in New York City and you're making a five-figure salary, you don't really get to save a lot of money. Your bank account is pretty much at zero right before your next paycheck is about to hit, so not having income tax taken out of my paychecks upon my move back to Florida started making a *big* difference in my life. For the first time I could ever remember, I was able to save money and dream of amenities that I couldn't afford while I was in New York City, like buying a house, which has always been one of my goals. I really felt like I leveled up as an adult with this move.

There were definitely some changes when I moved, as well. As we've established, I don't cook. I don't know how, and I really don't have any interest in it. (With that said, I'm Betty Crocker when it comes to baking, and I will happily whip up a bakery's worth of desserts in one night.) In fact, when my mom bought me a cooking class for the holidays, I asked her if I was on the naughty list that year, because it felt more like a punishment to be forced to learn how to cook than it did a gift.

In New York City, it's really expensive to cook for one person, because by the time you buy all the ingredients and seasonings you need for a recipe, you've broken the bank. Alternatively, I could pick up a six-dollar salad or sandwich, and it tasted way better than my cooking, anyway. Besides, New York truly has the best food and such a big variety of ethnic cuisines that I'd have been silly to cook even if I could have. Seamless became my best friend in the city. I could type in my zip code and see all the restaurants that delivered to my neighborhood, along with their menus. I also often met friends for dinner, so it would have been pointless to buy groceries, because I was out and about so much that they often went bad before I could eat them. Not to mention, the line to check out in New York City grocery stores often looks like everyone is getting the final supplies they need before a mass evacuation, and I had no car trunk to put the groceries in for the trip home. (On many occasions my bags broke open, and my groceries spilled onto the sidewalks and streets.) All in all, it was just better for everyone if the *food* came to *me*. So I pretty much ordered Seamless for most of my meals, and I had a ball! I'd order Italian food one night, Mediterranean the next, Thai food the following night, American the night after that, and then a Mexican fiesta to round out the week. It was basically as if Epcot came to me on a weekly basis.

But when I moved home to Tampa, there was no Seamless. I literally wondered—and asked—how people ever ate. Sure, I could order pizza or Chinese food to be delivered, but that was pretty much the extent of it. Or I could have gone to the grocery store, but what would I have done with what I bought there, anyway? As you might imagine, the food thing was a big adjustment for me.

I remember watching my boyfriend make Shake 'n Bake chicken one night. I thought, *Hey, that looks easy enough—even I could probably do that.* So I went to the store, bought a box of Shake 'n Bake and some chicken, and put the chicken in a pan with some oil (which I *swear* is what I thought I saw him do). One minute in, there was smoke, and my chicken very quickly became a blackened chicken finger. I texted him and asked, "Are you sure I cook this for 16 more minutes, the way the box indicates?" In his response he asked me what about the *bake* part of Shake 'n Bake didn't clearly indicate using the *oven*. I really just thought that *bake* meant going from one consistency to another, not the actual method of preparation. So there I was, with my apartment full of smoke and completely burned chicken that was supposed to have gone in the oven, and I was *frying* it. Maybe Shake 'n Bake chicken was too complicated for me, after all.

I also didn't have a dishwasher in any of my New York City apartments, so I bought the wrong kind of soap—the dish soap used for hand-washing dishes, not actual *dishwasher detergent*—and put it in the dishwasher and flooded my apartment during my first week back in Tampa. There were bubbles everywhere, and they went up to my knees. Clearly, this "being domestic" thing was off to a great start.

Thankfully, things were going slightly better on the work front. The company, because of its startup nature, was full of young people, and they became my first friends back in Tampa. I was so used to the constant hustle and bustle of New York City and being busy every minute of every day that it took some time to adjust to a quieter lifestyle. (Quiet is now my favorite setting.)

I've learned that when you move to any new city, it takes a year before it starts to feel like home. Be patient and give yourself time when you make drastic changes in your life. I had altered a lot—all at once—in my own life. Through my boyfriend, I also met friends who worked at the Lightning; and they, along with my new work colleagues, helped lay the foundation for my first adult friends back in Tampa.

Workwise, I was doing marketing and sales for the mobile startup in a hybrid role. At the time, I really missed sports and thought, *Oh no, I've left a big national market for a more local one, and I'm at a job that has nothing to do with sports. This feels like a dead end, and I'm never going to be able to get back into the sports world.* But I learned a valuable lesson in that role: no experience is a waste. You never know when what you learn or who you interact with is going to come back and benefit you. Years later, when I landed my first chief marketing officer position, I would've never been able to get that job if I hadn't gained all that mobile experience during this role. In fact, in the years after that job, everything became so mobile-centric, and my experience in the space gave me a major leg up.

You have to trust that you're where you're meant to be and that life has a way of working out for the best.

In the beginning of 2016, I experienced one of the worst time periods of my life—I broke up with my boyfriend and my dog died. We'd had Casey, a miniature poodle who could wave hello and goodbye and give high fives, for seventeen years. She was my first dog ever, we'd grown up together, and she was like a sibling to me. At the same time, I had to deal with the heartbreak of my relationship ending. I was so grief-stricken that I could barely brush my hair or get from one minute to the next. I was crying all the time, and I didn't think I'd survive that week. It was so much pain all at once, and the idea of ever finding happiness again seemed impossible.

At my mom's suggestion, I dragged myself to a therapist, who helped me start to heal. She taught me a curriculum's worth of advice about relationships that I've been able to pass along to many people in my own life. I often say that social media is a highlight reel and that when parents fight, they close the door, so you don't know what happened. We are taught all these clichés about life and don't learn about relationships in school, so how are we expected to know where the healthy boundaries lie?

Thank goodness my therapist taught me many essential lessons about what a healthy relationship looks like. I've been able to pass those tips along to my friends, and it's saved many of them in their own relationship decisions. I learned that relationships have the best chance of working out if you're with someone who's on the same intellectual and emotional maturity level and is your equal in the most fundamental areas. In addition, he also needs to consistently add to your emotional bank account, and it's much easier if he had the same fundamental upbringing. Finally, he has to be a "final sale" when he shows up (don't expect the person to change in any major categories).

It's almost as if the universe knew I was going through a really rough time and heard my yearning to get back into sports, because a few weeks later, I received a note from Gary Vaynerchuk's team. Gary's business partner, Stephen Ross, who also owned the Miami Dolphins and had invested in Vayner, was launching a new racial-equality startup called RISE (Ross Initiative in Sports for Equality). RISE was looking for a digital and social media person to join the company, and Gary recommended me for the role, which brings me to another important lesson in my life:

When Gary calls, I just say yes, and I know my life is about to change.

The one thing I knew about this particular chapter in my life was that I was really happy living in Tampa. I'd gone from prioritizing being busy all the time and accomplishing as much as possible in a day to really being the happiest when I was around sunshine, water, dolphins, and my family.

Team Gary and I thought that since the organization had been started by a Miami sports team owner, maybe I could stay in Florida to do the job. But after talking to the RISE team, I'd be the fifth employee, and the team really needed to all be in one place, which meant I had to move back to New York City. At first, I was still heartbroken over the breakup and the dog, so having my family as a support system nearby was comforting, and I'd pretty much decided that I was going to say no to the RISE job. But then I emailed Gary and asked for advice. He told me to make a list for him of the pros and cons of staying in Tampa versus moving back to New York City to take the job. When I sent him my list, he wrote back and said to take the RISE job. He was right.

As one of the handful of teachers I've ever had who really understands me, Gary is one of the very few people I have blind faith in. I know myself really well and typically circle back to my own point of view; but when Gary gives me advice, I know it's what's best for me, and I've always followed his guidance on major decisions.

I realized that no chapter is a waste. In hindsight, I learned a lot about relationships. I also unknowingly got to spend the last six months of my puppy's life with her, and I had dinner with my parents every Sunday night, if not more often. I wouldn't trade those experiences for the world. I thought a change of scenery at that point might be a healthy move for me.

Since I was still getting over so much loss, I wasn't functioning 100 percent on all cylinders. I needed to give RISE an answer about the job, and I had about a week to find an apartment. In an act of fate, I was scrolling through Facebook one day and saw a post from my dear friend Sam Sherman, who's one of the most quality people on the planet. I trust him implicitly. He had posted that his coworker, Kara Beaudet, was looking for a roommate in New York City. Coincidentally, the apartment was on the same avenue as the RISE offices, so I'd just have to walk seventeen blocks straight down in the morning to get to work. That seemed like a sign. In addition, Kara had an adorable dog named Riley, and some puppy love sounded really great at the time. If it hadn't been for Sam and Kara swooping in at that moment and making the final piece easy for me, I don't know that I would have been able to say yes to the job. Finding an apartment in New York City is a full-time job in itself, and I often say that if you can find one and get approved, you can do just about anything in life. I didn't have the energy then to go through that whole process, so those two really saved the day.

In March of 2016, I packed up my things again and headed back to New York City. Considering that I was in Tampa for six months, total, and that my time coincided with the winter months, I joked that I was the youngest snowbird ever that year. I was really getting a head start on the retirement lifestyle, except I was only twenty-nine years old!

## CHAPTER LESSONS

- Chase love and what your heart needs. Your personal life, happiness, and well-being deserve just as much weight in your life as your career ambitions.
- It's always better to give opportunities your best shot—even if you fail—than wondering, *What if?*
- When someone is meant to be in your life, you'll keep in touch and find ways to see each other, no matter the distance.
- Florida doesn't have any state income tax, which means that you get to take home a more significant portion of your paycheck compared to states that impose the tax.
- Your best chance to negotiate the factors that matter most to you is when you're starting a job. Make sure all your requirements are met up front. You don't have as much leverage once you're working for a company.
- I think the best way to increase your salary is to move around to different jobs every so often so that you're able to renegotiate your worth. As long as your story and job moves have a reasonable "why," recruiters will understand.
- You have to court employees the same way you would treat a relationship. If you take them for granted, they're going to leave you in the dust. And once a person has one foot out the door, it's too late to try and show him or her you care. That needed to be done while the person was in your presence and fully committed.

- When it says "bake," that it means it goes in the *oven*.
- When you move to a new city, it takes a year for it to start to feel like home.
- No experience is a waste. You learn valuable lessons and meet new people in everything you do. You have no idea at the time how those experiences may come back to help you later on.
- When you're struggling emotionally, therapy is there to help you. None of us can do life alone.
- Relationships have the best chance of working out if
    - you're with someone who's on the same intellectual and emotional maturity level;
    - the person is your equal in major categories;
    - your partner adds to your emotional bank account;
    - he or she had the same fundamental upbringing as you; and
    - your partner is a "final sale" when he or she shows up.
- Life usually works out the way it's supposed to.
- When Gary calls, just say yes and know that life is about to change.

# CHAPTER 8

# Sideline Racism

When I got back to New York City, I picked up exactly where I'd left off with my friendships. On the bright side, six months wasn't too much time to be away, so I still had many of my friends back in the city. It was as if I'd never left.

The best way to heal a broken heart is to fill it with love. And that's exactly what I did. On my first night back in New York, Lisa Diamond, a friend and one of my college roommates, invited me out to an event she was hosting. Having a place to go that night really helped save me from homesickness, as well as the heartbreak from which I was still reeling. (I'm pretty sure I cried the whole commute to and from the event.) But having laughs and smiles in between, thanks to Lisa, really helped ensure that my spirits were lifted as my New York City 2.0 chapter began.

That Monday, I started work at RISE.

RISE had the commissioner of every major professional sports league on its board and became the first organization to unite all the sports leagues for one cause. Talk about a shooting star of a dream job! The nonprofit also had every major news outlet on its board, as well as an advisory board of many of the top athletes across the sports world.

What I realized the minute I landed this job was that my passion was more than just sports. My heart was at the intersection of sports and making the world a better place, which Gary probably knew when he recommended me for the role. I was very motivated by the mission as I began my endeavor as RISE's first digital media manager. I was in charge of anything that happened with RISE and the Internet; so I oversaw the website, which we were still building at the time, as well as the social media accounts.

There's no doubt that trying to use the power of social media to eradicate racism was my greatest challenge yet.

This was my first job where there was no precedent. I couldn't turn to Johnny and say, "What did you do to get the message out about racial inequality in one hundred forty characters?" The task was on my shoulders. But it also presented an opportunity that I constantly reminded our team about: because we were one of the first organizations solely tackling this mission, we were leaders in this space. Everyone would be looking to us to take a stand and be the guides for how to react to and handle situations, as well as how to navigate this complicated issue.

My time at RISE coincided with the 2016 election, when Trump took office. No matter your political views, the election created a great divide in our country. While so many people went to work the next day sullen and feeling helpless (New York City was a ghost town the day after the election), I truly felt like I was exactly where I needed to be to do the work to make our world a better place.

I also felt like I was in my first job where I was directly making an impact on the world. After this experience, I could never go back to a job that was just for-profit and where my sole purpose was to help a company make money.

RISE was also my first job where the departments of the organization were so tightly knit together that one couldn't exist without the other. What I mean by that is that marketing is an amplification of what's happening at any organization. Potential clients and coworkers often want me to come into their companies and utilize marketing to help make them money, but it doesn't work like that. Marketing campaigns are an investment, so you need to have a budget. Marketing is also a megaphone for the initiatives happening within an organization, so without a foundation of who the company is and the real work it is doing, the company is not going to have successful marketing efforts.

I had truly never felt so impacted and moved as I was by the work we were doing at RISE. The team had created an implicit bias exercise, and I was told it was done with our board before I joined the team. Essentially, a list of people would be written on a piece of paper, and each person on the paper would be assigned a number. All you'd know was one fact about the person. So one woman was a CEO, a second worked at McDonald's, etc. You'd rank who you'd want to be, from most to least, numbered from one to eight. Then you'd find out a second fact about the person. Maybe the woman who was the CEO had a daughter with a serious illness. Or you'd learn that the guy who worked at McDonald's was actually part of a family who owned many franchises of the restaurant. Now that you knew a second fact about each person, you'd again rank who you would most want to be. Then you'd learn one final, third fact about the person and rank the list one more time.

Every time we did the exercise with a different group, people would look at their papers and gasp. Typically, people's ones through eights were not the same across the board. Each time you learned a new fact about a person, you'd change your mind about which person's life seemed most desirable to you. This happened to me, too, when I did the exercise. It really highlighted the fact that we all subconsciously judge books by their covers when we interact with people on a daily basis. Case in point: Right after I left the office the day I did the exercise, I got onto the subway. As people boarded the train, I knew that I would previously have made assumptions about the people walking onto the train without even meaning to. But since I'd just done the exercise, I caught myself thinking, *You really don't know anything about this person. Stop instantly making assumptions.*

RISE was already making me a better person.

I was at RISE not only during the 2016 election, but also as the Black Lives Matter movement was in the forefront of the news and when Colin Kaepernick kneeled during the national anthem. So I was on the front lines of working to help heal one of the nation's most pressing issues at the time.

We also hosted a tailgate before every Miami Dolphins game with law enforcement and the communities they served. I helped with the naming process, and we called those commUNITY Tailgates. Instead of neighborhoods being afraid of law enforcement or law enforcement officers misunderstanding members of their communities, we brought both groups together on an equal playing field that provided them with an opportunity to really get to know each other. As Gary V. always says, over-communication solves almost all problems. Facilitating over-communication between different parties on an issue in order to understand one another and unite was the theme of RISE. Week after week, I watched law enforcement officers hang out, laugh, and eat lunch with community members of all ages and form real connections. They also got to bond over the common ground of loving the Miami Dolphins.

No matter your age, gender, income, educational level, or socio-economic status, everyone looks up to athletes as heroes. So sports was the perfect vehicle to utilize as a platform to get out the message of unity. Athletes and sports leagues don't fully know they have the power to change the world. Even if you're the fourth-string punter on a team, you are a celebrity to fans. So when athletes use their platform for the greater good, they can make a tremendous impact in moving the needle on serious issues.

RISE also held town halls across the country that featured one athlete from each pro sports team in the city and the chief of police in that community. For example, we did one in Detroit, where we had an athlete representative from each major pro sports team in the city tell stories of what it was like to make it out of their neighborhoods growing up and the struggles they faced on a daily basis. You can't really understand someone else's life until you take a walk in their shoes.

Then, the police representative would speak, sharing that when they pull someone over, the first thing people often do is come up with a lie: "I was just heading to [someplace] and need to get there quickly. I left my ID at home…" Very rarely does someone roll down the window and say, "I'm sorry, officer, I was speeding and my taillight is burned out, so please hold me accountable for my actions." So often, the first impression people give them is false, which can make it difficult to trust. It made me realize that none of us is immune to the issues facing our country. We can all do better in our own lives to be more honest and accountable to help the overall issues happening in our world.

RISE also partnered with a number of players who chose to support our organization during the NFL's My Cause My Cleats initiative. During week 13 of the NFL season, the league allows players to wear cleats that represent a particular cause or foundation that has personal meaning to them. After the game, the cleats are auctioned off, and the money is donated back to that organization. A number of players across the league felt so strongly about our mission that they wanted to use the NFL's platform to fully support RISE. I came up with the name Sideline Racism for the campaign, so when week 13 hit and players on many teams stepped onto the field with their Sideline Racism cleats, it was one of the most meaningful moments of my career.

This was one of the first times that we had talked about an initiative in the office and online, and we saw it translate to tangible products in real life—on a major stage, nonetheless. Marketing campaigns are much more successful the more touch points you have, but many times, companies silo themselves into digital marketing or traditional marketing efforts. You're going to have the greatest success when you unite departments and figure out how you can get your unilateral message out in front of as many eyes and displayed in as many places as possible.

The NFL stage was so powerful that week that Draymond Green, who played for the Golden State Warriors, wanted to join in on the mission and the message. So he had basketball sneakers designed in a similar Sideline Racism format to the NFL players' and walked onto the court and played an NBA game in shoes that represented our organization. We now had two of the most major professional leagues spreading our message. It's hard to find a more powerful stage than that.

We also taught a racial equality curriculum in high schools across the country. RISE would host sessions called Train the Trainer, in which we'd bring in high school coaches who were participating in our program. Remember, sports were our vehicle across the board, and we stayed consistent with using that platform to convey our message of unity. So we'd train these high school coaches on our curriculum, and then, often instead of sports practice one day a week, they'd teach a new chapter of our curriculum to the kids on their teams. Now my favorite part: At the end of every semester, we'd get the kids together. Each school tended to be homogenous, based on the neighborhood it represented, and we'd host a big event for all the schools that participated in the curriculum that semester to come together.

I cried every time.

Kids from different neighborhoods, who likely would've never met each other if not for this program, were forming bonds and taking pictures with captions like "My new friends!" You could tell in that moment that a lot of these kids were going to be friends from then on and grow up together, which meant they'd be visiting each other's neighborhoods, resources would be going back and forth, new perspectives would be seen, and cycles would be broken. That's a good day at the office.

It's very difficult to change adults, because they kind of are who they are by that point in their lives. But kids are like sponges, and we knew we were opening these students' minds and giving them a new perspective that would change how they lived the rest of their lives.

I had my own eye-opening experiences during these events. First of all, even well-intentioned people are never taught how to talk about race, so one of the conversations that could best unite us and allow us to share what makes each of us unique is never broached. To avoid any awkwardness, people avoid those questions and conversations completely, even though they could potentially allow us to connect with one another. Secondly, and more personally, I felt very guilty for how I'd lived my life up until this point, unintentionally. I realized that most of us live in our own bubbles. We go about our days thinking about what we need and how we can enhance our own lives. We hang out with people who are just like us and don't want to go to *that neighborhood* over there because it's "dangerous and scary." Guess what? A lot of the people *there* don't want to be there either, but they need help to get out. Within our own cities, there are typically areas that are considered good areas and bad areas. These cities are our homes. Instead of just thinking about ourselves in the course of a day, what can we do to help our fellow neighbors who might need assistance and resources?

So much of any job is paying attention to what's happening in the world around you at any given time and how that can impact the work you are doing and the actions you need to take. I'm a news junkie, as we've discussed; so as I was reading through some of the top news and sports stories one day, I learned of a youth football team out of Texas called the Beaumont Bulls. They had seen Colin Kaepernick kneel during the national anthem and really related to him and viewed him as their hero, so they, too, decided to kneel when "The Star Spangled Banner" played during their own football game. There was a lot of backlash from their decision. People began saying really horrendous things and launching vicious threats at these kids who were only ten to twelve years old. After all the press, the league folded to the pressure and canceled the team's season.

If you're a middle-school-aged kid whose football hero stands up for a cause he believes in, and that cause is yours, as well, and you follow suit in taking a stand, and then you get punished for what you think is doing the right thing—just imagine the toll that must take on you at such a tender age!

I couldn't stand it, so I sent the article around to the RISE team and said we had to do something about it. We existed to assist in moments such as these. *This was our battle to fight.*

Luckily, every year at the Super Bowl, we'd hold our biggest town hall of the year, with players from across the NFL. We'd broadcast that town hall on various media outlets; and in an act of fate, the Super Bowl was in Houston that year—within driving distance of the Beaumont Bulls.

I am so proud and grateful that the RISE team recognized that we needed to jump into action to help with this situation. I spent a lot of time tracking down the coach on social media. I wasn't giving up until we got his contact information. Once I did so, I passed it along to the RISE team, and we invited the Bulls to join us at the town hall that year. The day of the event, in walked some of the top stars in the NFL, along with the Beaumont Bulls' coach and many of the team members. At the end of the event, the Beaumont Bulls and their coach came up to the front of the room, and the NFL players all stood up, shook hands with the kids on the team, hugged them, and told the kids how proud they were of them for standing up for what they believed in. These kids went from feeling punished for standing up for their beliefs to having their biggest heroes praise them for their actions. We took a group picture of the NFL players and the Beaumont Bulls team. Every time I look at that picture, I still get teary eyed because when those kids left that room, they felt reassured that standing up for what they believed in really does pay off after all.

In addition, something happened after that that I couldn't have imagined in my wildest dreams: a group of the NFL players decided to help fund an entirely separate league with the best equipment and resources you could imagine. So in a matter of weeks, these kids went from feeling like they had been kicked to the curb to having NFL players on their side, picking *them*. The Beaumont Bulls quickly became the envy of all the other kids who knew them. That's another great day at the office and exactly why I could never go back to a job that's just about making money.

I also had the opportunity to help design an ad in the Super Bowl program to represent RISE. We found out at the last minute that we had the ad space and had only a few days to pull off the project. Vayner to the rescue! I reached out to James Orsini, who's been part of the VaynerMedia leadership team since I worked for the company. James has also been an incredible friend, advocate, and supporter; and any time I've reached out to him for help, he's always jumped right on it and steered me to the right person or found the best way to help me accomplish my goal. James has always treated me like family, even since I left VaynerMedia.

When we realized we had this unique opportunity on the biggest stage, I knew James would find a way to help me get the job done and would be willing to deploy all resources necessary to help with the project. So we worked together with Vayner and came up with an amazing ad that showed the faces of two football players; instead of just one line of eye black on the players' faces, there were *two* lines, which created an equals sign under the players' eyes, along with the copy "Equality is a winning play." The final product was truly breathtaking and a really creative approach for getting our message out properly, given the stage, and in a way that would really catch fans' attention at the game.

Another perk of having an ad in the program meant that the organization received two Super Bowl tickets as part of the package. *Ahh!!!!!!* That was me screaming when I found out. Because after I crossed off seeing Oprah live from my bucket list, my next number-one goal was to attend the Super Bowl. And here it was, finally happening; all of my hard work was paying off. Since I'd been in charge of bringing the ad to life, I naturally assumed that I was going to get those tickets. That is, until I learned that the organization was allocating them to some people our CEO had decided upon. I was devastated—but not deterred. I simply made a decision that I was still going to find a way to go to the game.

We had our "It Takes All Colors" photo-booth activation at the NFL Experience in Houston, and the inclusive and true definition of a leader, Erin Pellegrino, always made a case of why I should be at these events for marketing purposes and about the work I'd done to help bring our activations to life. Erin oversaw our events department and worked collaboratively with the other departments to bring RISE's mission to life through our events. She also made sure to include everyone who participated in helping plan the events as part of the final experience. As I said, she embodies leadership.

So I was partway to Houston, with my flight and hotel paid for. I wasn't going to go that far and get that close to my dream and *not* make it happen. *Hello, have you met me yet?*

While I was in Houston, I saw a listing on Facebook from someone who was selling a Super Bowl ticket. He had many pictures at sporting events, reviews on what a great ticket seller he was, and an official business. We met in person in a very public and crowded establishment in Houston, and I purchased the ticket from him. We spent about an hour talking and then went our separate ways.

I was so excited to share with everyone who texted me that week that I'd landed a ticket to the big game, and they were all ecstatic for me, as they knew how much going to the game meant to me. The morning of the Super Bowl, the ticket seller texted me to ask if I was excited and suggested I purchase a plastic ticket holder to make sure the ticket would be secure. As soon as my work responsibilities ended that day, I sprinted to an Uber and headed off to the stadium. I did notice on that car ride that the writing on the back of my ticket was a little blurry. I texted the seller about it, and he said that that sometimes happens when tickets are printed. I later learned that was a major red flag, but I didn't know any better at the time.

When I got to the stadium, I went through security and waited outside for the ticket seller to show up. (He told me that we were sitting together at the game and to meet him outside the gates, and we could walk in together.) While I was waiting for him, I noticed that my ticket was slightly wider and longer than the tickets of the other people walking into the game. I texted him about this, as well, and he assured me that the ticket would work just fine, and I was going to the game. As kickoff neared and the sun began to set, I was still waiting for him outside. He constantly kept me posted, saying, "I'm thirty minutes away . . . fifteen minutes away . . . I'll be there at five fifteen," etc.

Just a few minutes from kickoff, I realized I'd been conned and that he wasn't showing up. I knew in my gut that the ticket was probably a fake, but I still walked up to the ticket scanner hoping for the best. The ticket taker confirmed my worst fear: the ticket wasn't real. I texted the seller to tell him that I knew what he'd done to me and that I would be taking appropriate action. He tried to tell me that his ticket didn't work either and that we needed to "find the person who sold us the fake tickets"!

*Yeah right, buddy. I'm not dumb. That was you.*

Completely dejected and feeling at rock bottom, I burst into tears. Through my tears, I had a bittersweet moment, a beautiful and perfect view of the flyover after the national anthem, unobstructed by crowds because I was the only one still standing outside watching. I did, however, miss the women from *Hamilton* singing "America the Beautiful." I asked all the fans walking in if they had an extra ticket. Spoiler alert: *No one has extra tickets to the most epic event of the year.*

So, with my head hanging very low and tears streaming down my face, I began walking away from the stadium, figuring I'd grab an Uber when I was in a more accessible location.

As I was walking away, I saw a police officer driving by in a golf cart. I have no idea what possessed me to do this, but I stopped him, hopped in his golf cart, told him my story, and asked if he'd drive me around the stadium to see if we could find a ticket. He took pity on me, and off we went to the StubHub tent, where they said something along the lines of "Are you kidding? There *are* no extra tickets to the Super Bowl!" We then went to the NFL tent, where I was told that they couldn't help me. They even took my fake ticket away, so I no longer had proof of what had happened to me.

Feeling totally knocked down by that experience and the fact that we'd driven completely around the stadium only to come up empty-handed, I asked the officer if he could just drive me to the edge of the stadium to a safe location, somewhere without a bunch of random people around who didn't get into the game, so that I could call for a ride home. As we were driving through the parking lot to the edge of the stadium, I said to him, "You know what? I have one more idea I could try. Stay here for one second—I just have to know that I left it all on the field before I give up and go home."

I texted RISE's CEO, knowing that she was sitting in Steve Ross's suite, and let her know the situation. She said she was so sorry that this had happened and was going to see what Mr. Ross could do to help. By then, it was the middle of the game, and she texted back that there was nothing that could be done at this point on her end and suggested I reach out to Troy Vincent, the executive vice president of football operations for the NFL. He was also our RISE contact at the league office and attended our board meetings. Luckily for me, since I worked in social media, I knew from spending so much time on Twitter that Troy was also awesome at utilizing Twitter.

I thought, *An NFL executive isn't going to read my tweet in the middle of the NFL's biggest event of the year, but I guess I have nothing to lose.*

I took a chance and sent him a tweet letting him know the circumstances of what had happened. He instantly wrote me back—which blew me away—and told me to head back to the NFL area and ask for one of his colleagues. Mind you, these were the people who had closed the window on me previously and told me there was nothing they could do to help. But what did I have to lose at this point?

The officer, who was basically like family by then, drove me back to the NFL window in his golf cart and waited while I gave this new opportunity a try. As the NFL ticket folks lifted up the window, they were probably thinking, *Great, this girl again.* I handed them the phone (through tears, because I don't think I'd stopped crying since the disappointment of my fake ticket) and let them know that Troy had sent me their way. They took my phone to review the conversation and asked me some questions to confirm that I really worked at RISE. *I passed the test, obviously!* They asked why I hadn't told them that I worked at RISE the first time I came to see them. I told them it was my own fault that I'd bought a ticket that wasn't real, and I wasn't going to involve my employer when the company had nothing to do with it.

The responsibility fell solely on me, and I wouldn't name-drop to try to fix a problem. *I'd* messed up, and it was *my* fault.

They took my phone and closed the window. I thought, *Great, they already confiscated my ticket. Now my phone, too?* They finally gave me my phone back, closed the window, and huddled inside the office. While I stood there for what felt like forever, unsure of what was happening inside that ticket office and tortured by the sounds of people cheering inside the stadium while they lived out *my* dream, the window finally opened once again after about ten minutes.

I will never forget the words that came next. The guy behind the ticket window handed me a ticket (a *real* one this time!) and said, "This one is on us. Enjoy the game!" The ticket, since it came from the league, ended up being in the NFL *family section*, which was an even better seat than the "ticket" I'd originally purchased.

I burst into tears, thanked him profusely, then went and hugged the officer (my new best friend from the day) and told him the good news. He couldn't believe it either! Then I ran into the stadium like I was Rudy running onto the field for the first time.

Here's the thing about me: Even when there is no hope, and I am at complete rock bottom, I still don't give up. There has to be not a single option or idea left on the planet for me to walk away and throw in the towel.

The game was between the Atlanta Falcons and New England Patriots. While I'd been stuck outside as the game began, hearing the cheers inside had completely crushed my soul. But when I ran into the game in the second quarter, the Falcons were up 14–0. The game would eventually go into overtime, with the Patriots making an epic comeback to win 34–28. So I didn't really miss any of the major football action. I made it into the stadium just in time for the comeback, and I got to my seat before Lady Gaga's halftime show. This particular Super Bowl was also the first game that Tom Brady's mom attended after battling cancer that season. So despite my debacle leading up to the game, I didn't really miss a single magical moment. In addition, I kept running into people at the stadium who'd seen me stuck outside and were overjoyed that I'd made it into the game. It was like a big family inside the stadium that night.

Since I'd done so much texting and talking on the phone while trying to sort out the ticket chaos prior to the game, by the time the last bit of confetti fell and I had to leave the stadium, my phone's battery was at 1 percent. I had no cash on me, and the line to hail an Uber was over an hour long, which meant that, by the time I reached the front of the line, my phone would be dead and I wouldn't be able to get a ride home. Once again, I found myself stuck in the parking lot of this darn stadium!

I was sharing my story from the night with some nice Patriots fans standing behind me in the Uber line, and they actually handed me their portable phone charger and let me charge my phone the entirety of the hour-long line. The kindness of strangers! Looking back at that night, I experienced the highest of highs and the lowest of lows, but I attended my first Super Bowl ever and made it back to my hotel safely!

I did file a police report the next day about my fake ticket, but on the bright side, my resilience and determination reached a new high that night. I really proved the impossible to myself, and I got to check the number-one item off of my bucket list. Today, when something feels impossible, I look back at that night as motivation and remind myself of what I was able to pull off.

That was certainly one of the highlights of my time at RISE. But shortly after I moved to New York City to begin my job with the organization, we learned that there was going to be a management change. We were told that the new management might retain the current staff—but then again, maybe not. *Déjà vu!* There I was again, having just signed a year lease in the Big Apple, and once again I was hit with the potential of not having a job. I had to think fast. I was also getting sick of giving my all to a job, being very passionate about the work, and then having someone else control my fate.

I was ready to have a backup plan. No matter what happened to my jobs throughout my life, I didn't want to keep being left high and dry; and I knew that if I started my own business, no one could take that away from me.

A few months into my time back in New York City, a friend introduced me to her fiancé, who also worked in sports. As we sat down for lunch, he began telling me that his company needed some social media help and asked if I'd come in and talk to his team about social media and give them some guidance. I was happy to help him, and we set a day for me to meet with his team.

Finally, the day arrived for me to meet some of the executives at his sports agency and begin telling them the strategies and tips for using social media wisely in order to help build a brand. The meeting went very well, and they asked me if I could put together a social media strategy for Phil Mickelson. I said, "Sure, no problem!"

So I went home, launched a company, which I named Social Victories, and Googled social media contracts. I put one together and had my dad, Steve, a business lawyer (and still Social Victories' lawyer to this day), review it and sign off on it.

I spent every waking hour that weekend working on the social media game plan for Phil. It covered everything from platform overviews to best practices, social media sponsorships, and strategies on how to effectively run social media ads. The game plan took me thirty hours and was twenty pages long. I sent it off to the team, and they absolutely loved it! They were blown away and didn't have a single point of negative feedback.

After some challenging experiences with bosses who micromanaged my work, I'd almost been broken down and disregarded my worth. I'd completely forgotten what I was capable of and that the work I did had value and could be really appreciated by clients.

I liked this new feeling. It was a huge weight off my shoulders to be able to control the destiny of my work, without having bosses criticize the advice I so strongly believed in. Even better, clients were agreeing with the recommendations I was making.

I learned another important lesson during that time: When you have a skill set, but you're working for another company, no one thinks to hire you or utilize those skills. But the minute you go out on your own and launch a company around that skill set, people instantly see you as the expert in that area. They think to hire you only *once you're actually up for hire* and you're openly taking on clients.

I realized that, even with as many years as I'd been doing social media, no one had thought to hire me for the needs of their companies. But the minute I went out on my own, clients started lining up. Sometimes you have to be the one to take the first leap of faith to create opportunities for yourself. Before launching my own company, people just knew that I was applying my skill set to the corporations for which I worked. But when I went out on my own, they then saw that as the green light to send projects my way. You really never know who needs help in a particular field until you start letting people know you can assist. I would've had no idea that the clients who started coming my way needed social media help until they knew I was available and willing to help. I was now spending a large percentage of my waking hours working compared to when I had first moved to the city.

Basically, I was paying New York City rent and not really utilizing much of what the city had to offer. I also had a decent number of friends who'd started to move away from the city. When I first moved to New York, I was twenty-four years old. The friends I'd met were in the same stage of life, and we were always out doing activities together. Six years later, I was nearing thirty, and our priorities were just different. A number of close friends began getting married and migrating out of the city.

As we've discussed, absolutely no chapter is a waste. That year in New York City, I got to attend birthday parties, go on outings with Vayner friends, and even lived on a boat and visited Croatia for a week during the summer. I attended both the Pac-12 basketball and gymnastics championships and got to see the *CBS Evening News* live— thanks to my friend Susan Helvenston, who worked at the network. My dear friend and RISE coworker Stephon Preston and I got to see Andy Cohen's Bravo show in person, and I went apple picking at orchards and to pumpkin patches in the fall, both of which were some of my favorite activities while living up north. I also saw my favorite Broadway show, *Dear Evan Hansen*, with my roommate Kara. And I went to the Super Bowl and saw *Hamilton* in the same week! Needless to say, my year back in New York City was anything *but* a waste, and it was filled with some of the absolute best memories of my life.

But still, every time I'd go home to Tampa, when it was time to leave, I'd hold on to the car door on the way to airport and say, "Mom, please just tell me I don't have to go back." As much fun as I had in New York, my heart was still in Tampa.

And once again, the universe heard me. I'd let Gary know at some point during the year that I missed Tampa. And one day, I was sitting in my office and the phone rang. It was Gary. I didn't recognize the number, and I was on the phone with another Vayner employee at the time, catching up, so the call went to voicemail. When I listened to the message, it was Gary asking me to call him.

And what have we learned? When Gary calls, just say yes. I knew my life was about to change.

## Chapter Lessons

- The best way to heal a broken heart is to fill it with love.
- When you are the first in any space, the world is going to look to you as a leader and watch how you handle issues.
- After landing a job where I was making a direct impact on the world, there was no going back to a role where the sole goal was to generate revenue for a company.
- Marketing is an amplification, or megaphone, of what's happening at an organization.
- You need to look at marketing as an investment, which means a marketing budget is required to amplify your company successfully.
- When you run into people you don't know on a daily basis, stop making assumptions about them. Unless you really get to know them, you have no idea who they truly are or what's happening in their lives.
- Another Gary V. lesson: Over-communication solves almost all problems.
- You really can't understand someone else's life until you take the time to take a walk in his or her shoes.
- We can all do better in our own lives to be more honest and accountable in order to help move the needle on the issues facing our country.
- Marketing efforts will be much more successful when you display your message in multiple locations so that consumers see it in many parts of their lives.
- We all live in our own bubble and typically hang out with people who are just like us. Let's ask ourselves how we can help those in our own communities—our neighbors—who might need some assistance and resources that we can provide. Also,

you really learn a lot and grow as a person when you hang out with people who are different from you. We can all expand our horizons.

- When it seems as if all options are exhausted while striving for a goal, keep going and try to find a solution, until there is not a single possibility left on the planet.
- When you have a skill set but are working for a particular company, clients don't see you as being available to help them. It's not until you take the first leap of faith and let people know you have your own company that they think to hire you for their needs.

# CHAPTER 9

# CMO for One NFL Player

I had no idea what Gary had up his sleeve. He's so busy that you don't want to miss his calls, and I didn't know when I'd be able to connect with him again. To this day, I still have his voicemail saved on my phone because I'd known then it was bound to be a life-changing call.

I immediately called him back, and—of course—his phone rang and then went to voicemail. *Great, he's probably on the way to Australia,* I thought. I hung around the office for a few hours, not wanting to be on the subway when he called back. Then I thought, *I can't stay here all night. I have to go home at some point.* I made the seventeen-block trek back to my apartment safely without getting a call from him underground. As dinnertime came and went without a phone call, I grew more anxious. *Does he have good news or bad news for me?*

As someone who plays out every scenario in her head and can run through all the possibilities of a situation the way a computer browser can have a hundred tabs open at once, I truly had no idea of what he had in store for me. But my heart was beating fast thinking about it. I definitely do not like the unknown. *At all.*

Finally, later that evening, the phone rang, and Gary's name popped up on the caller ID.

*Here we go.*

Gary is famous for holding meetings in three- to six-minute increments. He says that if you block out thirty minutes or an hour for a meeting, you'll waste time using up that entire slot because you know you have that amount of time blocked off on your calendar. However, if you book meetings for only a few minutes, you'll be more efficient and get everything you need to say across as quickly as possible, knowing you only have the person's attention for a short time.

Case in point: I knew this was going to be a quick call, but there'd be a big bomb dropped in there.

Gary, who'd known I wanted to move back to Tampa, told me that NFL wide receiver Brandon Marshall, who'd most recently played for the New York Jets (Gary's favorite team and the team he wants to buy one day), was looking for a marketing person for his personal brand and businesses, which included a mental-health nonprofit and a line of fitness centers.

Gary was recommending me for the job.

*Phew, this call was good news!*

I, of course, was appreciative that he'd think of me again for such a cool opportunity. Furthermore, Gary told me that Brandon was looking for someone who was located in either New York, where Brandon was playing; Chicago, where his nonprofit was based; or Florida, where his main gym was located. If you do the math and carry the one, that meant I could move back to Tampa! *Hallelujah!* I never knew what job it would be that would allow me to move back home, where I wasn't also sacrificing all I'd built in my career. But six years after I'd left home (so much for living in New York City for one year), I finally had my answer.

In my current role at RISE, I was working with every major sports league. My one question for Gary was, Wasn't it going to be a drop off for me to go from that portfolio to working for *one single athlete* in *one* sport? It seemed like I would be losing the ability to connect with many different leagues and athletes if I made this move.

But, of course, Gary's response was another teachable moment. He said that he had always thought I had entrepreneurial tendencies and that the work I was doing for RISE was forever going to benefit the organization and the founder. Basically, all of my innovations and successes anytime I worked for a company would be attributed to the organization as a whole. However, everything I did in working for Brandon would be the direct result of *my* efforts, and I would be the one getting noticed for the work I was doing. Essentially, Gary believed in me and felt that I deserved credit for the results I was generating.

*It made so much sense.*

Gary's team gave me a few more details about Brandon's companies and then passed my information along to Brandon, and I waited to hear from him. Once we hopped on the phone, we instantly hit it off and had a great conversation. I found him to be very down-to-earth. It was such a thrilling moment for me, as I'd spent my entire life idolizing football players. And here I was, in talks to work for one. I had to pinch myself. After a few more text messages throughout the next week, we decided to make it official. Brandon texted me and said, "Let's build something great by building each other up," which is really how every relationship dynamic should go.

And off we went. Brandon gave me the title of chief marketing officer, or CMO. From what one of my contacts at the NFL told me, I was the first CMO he had heard of working for one single NFL player. Again, like relationships, you can't always predict your next job; you just know it when you see it. How could I have ever dreamed of this role when, from what friends had told me, I was the first one they'd ever heard of doing it?

Shortly after I found out I'd gotten the job, I gave my two weeks' notice at RISE and immediately booked my one-way ticket home to Tampa. RISE wanted me to work the full two weeks, and by the time the contracts with Brandon were done, we were 1.9 weeks away from my start date, so my last day at RISE was also my first day in my new role. I was also moving back to Tampa, and Wi-Fi was being installed in my apartment that day, so it was a quite a day.

Once again, prioritize what's most pressing and what your heart needs the most. Tampa was the answer for me, and so was finally being able to captain my own ship.

I really want to emphasize that you never have to settle. You can have the dream job without sacrificing quality of life. I live in paradise in Tampa; I experience sun, water, pro sports, and eighty-degree temperatures regularly, and I get to see my family multiple times a week. Sometimes, I'll be on the phone and say, "Can you please hold? I'm watching dolphins."

The timing was also perfect in that my lease was up in Manhattan, as I'd been in New York exactly a year during this 2.0 chapter. I'd successfully survived the change in CEOs while still being able to maintain my full-time job and pay my year's rent.

Brandon ended up signing with the New York Giants a few months after we began working together.

In my role as CMO, I was in charge of Brandon's endorsement deals and personal brand, as well as the marketing for his mental-health nonprofit and fitness centers. I was the only person within his organization working for all three companies at one time. It kind of felt like raising three kids simultaneously. There was at least one company that had pressing needs at any given time, and everyone else worked within only one of the organizations.

Brandon was diagnosed with borderline personality disorder while he was playing in the NFL. Many people close to him told him not to tell anyone, as it might hinder his chance at another contract and put a damper on his career. Instead, he decided to hold a press conference in 2011, announcing his diagnosis to the world. Talk about bravery.

I have been told that athletes and minorities are two groups that stereotypically don't talk about vulnerabilities. So the fact that he was both really made him a pioneer and face of the mental-health movement for so many demographics. He knew that, in holding his press conference, if he was brave enough to break the stigma and talk about his mental-health challenges, so many others would feel brave enough to follow suit and get the help they needed.

Within the organization, we went around the country and held Youth Mental Health First Aid trainings, which are designed to ultimately help adolescents experiencing mental-health crises. To me, they felt very much like suicide-prevention trainings. We conducted sessions all across the country with adults who worked with children, and taught them the signs to look for when someone is in mental-health distress and the steps to take to get the youths the help they need.

Working for Brandon's mental-health nonprofit was really eye-opening for me and drove home the fact that you cannot be your best self without your physical and mental well-being being intact.

The conversation around mental health really burst onto the scene right around the time I began working for Brandon. Many meditation apps emerged and became mainstream just as I was beginning this job, so I was once again working on an issue that seemed to be at the center of the universe, as it was incredibly pressing and important to our culture.

One particular trend I took notice of was that clusters of suicides seemed to be happening in privileged communities. Often, in these situations, kids would feel they couldn't live up to their parents' expectations or compete against their peers. We'd have a much healthier society if, instead of telling kids there's one way to succeed—by getting As in these certain five subjects—we would simply figure out what their strengths are and create a path more tailored to their interests so that they feel good about themselves from an early age.

I felt like I went from oblivion to awareness on the topic of mental health while I was in this job. It had just never been brought to my attention. And what I realized in this role is that we are all affected by the topic. Every person is somewhere on the mental-health spectrum, and the more work we put in to improve our mental well-being, the healthier we will be.

Also, I realized that hurt people hurt people. If people treats you less than wonderfully, kindly, supportively, and with openness, they most likely don't feel good about themselves, so don't take their actions personally. They have their own insecurities to deal with. The better the place we are in mentally, the better we treat others. So working on yourself is actually the greatest gift you can give to those around you.

It's important to know that you're not alone. Whatever you're feeling, a hundred people around you are likely feeling the same thing. You just don't realize it. And whatever you're going through at any given time probably has a name, and there is likely a solution out there to help you. I repeat: Whatever you're struggling with mentally and emotionally is probably incredibly common and often the norm, and there are mainstream resources out there to assist you through this time. No one is dealt four aces in life. Everyone has their struggles. But on the flip side, it never rains forever, and you'll get through this rough patch.

I once heard this quote somewhere, and I think it's a major key to life: "In order to experience the greatest happiness, you really need three things at all times in life: someone to love, something to do, and something to look forward to." That trifecta should be the North Star.

And in the "something to do" category, I'd hit the jackpot of dream jobs. In the roles I'd held up until this point, I was always making decisions or suggestions for organizations, but I was many layers removed from the actual action. In this job, I was finally able to make direct suggestions for how an athlete should build his brand.

In my role working for Brandon, I helped increase donations to his mental-health nonprofit by utilizing all the technology and first-mover tactics I'd learned in my roles up until this point. For example, I donated my thirtieth birthday to his nonprofit when Facebook fundraisers first came on the scene. My own birthday raised $2,813 just on Facebook, and overall, the fundraisers brought in thousands of dollars for the organization. People donated birthdays, bat mitzvahs, holidays, and all different occasions. It was so amazing to watch people believe in our mission so much that they became ambassadors and selflessly wanted to donate their occasions to support our cause.

I also helped get Brandon on a new texting platform when it first came out, and he became one of the first NFL players who put a cell phone number out there where fans could text him. We received over forty thousand messages just in the first month or so. And while fans were waiting for a reply, we directed them to the Facebook fundraiser link, which nearly fifteen hundred people clicked on to consider donating their occasion to our cause. We had Snapchat filters for the first time and ping-pong GIFs at his yearly fundraiser that fans could share directly on their social media channels, all to bring awareness and help to further brand his nonprofit. Both Brandon and the nonprofit also participated in mental-health Twitter chats to facilitate open dialogue on the subject of mental health and to allow a celebrity to join in with the masses. We also redid the website; and, instead of just asking for money, we listed the different products people could purchase to support the foundation. You could spend only $6.50 and donate a mental-fitness toolkit to a group of kids, or pay more and donate training to a group of adults, or even have Brandon come speak to your organization. The point was that, instead of just sending a random donation to a foundation, with no idea of what would actually happen to it, we focused on making sure there were donation levels for every budget and that you knew exactly where your money was headed once you made the donation. That way, you knew your money was going to directly impact someone who needed it. With all the work we did, donations increased quite a bit in 2017, which made me so happy, knowing we were going to be able to reach and assist more people who needed mental-health help.

We also collaborated with Bose to create headphones that exactly matched Brandon's cleats during My Cause My Cleats so that he had multiple items that represented his foundation to showcase that week. We did partnerships with the Players' Tribune, a favorite outlet of mine for its positive storytelling and support of athletes, in order for Brandon to tell the story of his mental-health journey. One of our goals was working to break the stigma surrounding open and honest conversations around mental health. Although it never came to life, one of my favorite ideas I pitched was to create life-sized letters that spelled out the word STIGMA. But we would remove the *I*, and as people walked by, they could take a photo standing where the *I* would've been. We'd then have a photo-booth activation put the words "I break the stigma," over the photo, since the person would've physically been breaking up the word. They would be getting the message out that they were brave enough to stand up and break the stigma and were willing to have open conversations about mental health.

One of my favorite activations we did with Brandon was on his first game ever with the Giants, against the Dallas Cowboys. We created an Instagram story of the playlist Brandon would be listening to on the field as he warmed up. Remember, access is the best form of content. And fans want as much behind-the-scenes access to their favorite athletes as they can get. As much as TV networks show the players warming up with headphones on the field before a game, we never know what music is motivating them. So we wanted to change that and give fans a little more insight. Thanks to VaynerMedia once again, who brought our vision to life with amazing animations, we created graphics that zoomed in on a map to show where Brandon was warming up that day and where the stadium was located. We then proceeded to post his playlist in the order he was listening to the songs during warm-ups. Fans went *wild*. Again, it's just about being a first-mover and providing value where people's eyes are located, which was on Instagram stories. Each song card got forty thousand to fifty thousand views. And that was all free to post. Totally free ad space.

On the gym front, when I arrived, there were many pro athletes working out in Brandon's facility, but the goal was to open the gym more to the general public and host additional classes for the everyday gym goer. The general public had never had much access to work out alongside their heroes, which would be a dream to most people. So I suggested we use the tagline "Train like the Pros." This message made it clear to pro athletes that we provided everything they needed for a world-class workout experience, while locals would get access to the same facilities, equipment, trainers, and resources as the top athletes in the country. It was the perfect tagline to accomplish our mission.

We also brought in a nutritionist during my time with the gym, so patrons could have someone help them with grocery shopping, meal planning, and meal prep. You give yourself the best chance of accomplishing your goals when your nutrition plan is working hand in hand with your workout routine. We created all new brochures, organized our offerings into clear categories with recognizable class names, revamped the website, joined ClassPass and Groupon, created a content pillar of our social media that was geared toward educational posts, launched sports-specific-training social media posts, and created a beautiful Combine brochure for athletes and agents who were selecting NFL Combine training programs ahead of the NFL Draft. We saw double-digit increases on a number of our social media platforms.

All of this happened in less than a year. It was a marathon, but I was so proud of all the work we'd accomplished across the board. I learned a ton, and when I looked back, all of the entities were in much better shape than when I started, and I was very proud of that fact. When you are working for three entities at once and reporting to a bunch of difference bosses, it makes it hard to take a day off. I'm not sure I ever did that year. I even continued working while evacuating from a hurricane that was headed straight for Tampa. Luckily, the direct hit missed us, and everything was still standing when I returned. But it turns out hurricane season and football season do coincide, so I had to make sure the show went on.

Speaking of the perfect storm . . . A few games into Brandon's tenure with the Giants, during week 5 of the season, he hurt his ankle and had to be carted off the field. The injury required season-ending surgery, which brought his twelfth year in the NFL to a close. Off-the-field opportunities stem from a player's success in the spotlight, so that was certainly a blow to all of our initiatives. Athletes learn great skills in the team-building and leadership arenas on the field; but when it comes time for business, you need to equip yourself with a team of people who are well versed in marketing, HR, operations, legal, accounting, etc. It truly takes a village of skill sets to run a business. With Brandon not playing on the field for months by the time early 2018 hit, he certainly didn't need a full-time person running his endorsement deals anymore. My work for Brandon's company ended in January of 2018.

I had finally found my dream job, and I was forever changed by the work we did in the mental-health space. I consider that education such a life-changing gift. I also learned a ton about the fitness industry and athlete endorsement deals and became an even better chief marketing officer than when I started the job.

But now that my supposed dream job had come to a close, what next?

## Chapter Lessons

- Gary V. often held meetings in three- to six-minute increments. If you schedule thirty minutes or an hour for a meeting, you'll typically take up that entire timeframe because you know you have it blocked off on your calendar. However, if you schedule meetings to be just a few minutes long, you'll use your time to convey your message more efficiently, knowing your time is limited.

- When you work for a company, the fruits of your labor are going to benefit the company as a whole, and the organization will receive the credit. When you're an entrepreneur, *you* get the credit for the successes you create.

- In any relationship dynamic, build something great by building each other up. One-sided relationships aren't healthy and won't succeed long-term.

- You don't have to settle in the category of quality of life. You can live in a place you love while also having your dream job. Don't give up until you've found both. I'm living proof that it is possible.
- You cannot be your most successful self without your physical and mental well-being functioning on all cylinders.
- We'd have a much healthier society if, instead of telling kids there's one way to succeed, we took the time to figure out what their strengths are and create a path more tailored to their interests so that they feel good about themselves.
- We are all affected by mental health. The more work each of us puts in to improve our mental well-being, the healthier we will be. Everyone is somewhere on the mental-health spectrum, and we all can do work every day to improve. There is no cap on how mentally healthy one can be.
- Whatever you're feeling at any given time most likely has a name, there are hundreds of other people around you feeling the same way, and there are resources out there to help you navigate what you're experiencing.
- To experience the greatest happiness life has to offer, I recommend always having someone to love, something to do, and something to look forward to.

# CHAPTER 10

# Energy Vampires

As 2018 began, I made a New Year's resolution to allow zero percent toxicity in my life. It's a lesson I teach to my clients and share with my friends, as well. Zero percent toxicity means eliminating anyone who brings you down and does very little to contribute to your emotional bank account or well-being. I call these people energy vampires.

Activities can be energy vampires, too. There are some things and people we keep around because that's just the way it's always been. However, I reached my highest level of happiness to date when I made the decision to eliminate the remaining toxicity in my life, because it trimmed out all of the "fat" that was holding me back on a daily basis. And while it may seem like you just *cannot* walk away from a relationship in your life that's a burden, the minute you actually do so, you're creating space for what you're meant for and something so much better. It's addition by subtraction.

And think of it this way: *If you don't stand up for yourself, who will?* Anyone who makes you uncomfortable or doesn't meet your personal standards is someone who has to be kept at arm's length. "Pleasant but distant" is a piece of advice I once got. Simply put: I know what I deserve, and anyone who doesn't meet those standards gets punted out of my life. When I care about someone, that person is family to me and gets all of me—my whole heart. That takes a lot of energy, so I reserve that gift for those who are 100 percent all in, devoted and loyal to me. Anyone who treats you poorly or makes you feel less than what you deserve is not an equal and is likely never going to be someone who adds to your emotional bank account.

Another lesson I learned from my therapist is that if you want something or someone in your life and the answer is currently either *no*, *I don't know*, *maybe*, or *I'm not ready*, the answer for now is *no*. There is only one answer that means yes, and that's when someone is all in and says, unequivocally, *yes*.

Your mental well-being is always too big a price to pay. If you're in a dynamic where you feel net negative at the end of every day, get out. No job, person, or amount of money is worth you being brought down or sacrificing feeling whole.

Because here's the thing: As a wise coworker once told me, people will do what you allow them to do. So *you* have to set the boundaries and be the bouncer of your own well-being.

Do your best to surround yourself with authentic people. They are the happiest and most confident people. One way to identify authentic people is that their actions exactly match how they feel. Whatever it is they're feeling inside, they tell you. It's vulnerability. They don't play games, they don't manipulate, they don't send mixed signals, they don't play you. They are real, honest, all-in, and usually make your life the happiest when you're around them. They make you feel comfortable *being the first you*. Find them, cherish them, and don't let them go. I always want to know how someone feels about me and where they stand in my life. Authentic people are confident in their feelings and expressive about them.

In that vein, pay attention to people's actions, not just their words. *People are their actions*. So, regardless of what people tell you, what do their actions say? Your answer lies within how they are behaving. I also suggest not making permanent decisions on temporary people.

Energy vampires come in all forms and ingratiate themselves in all parts of our day. One example is the number of text messages that have taken over our lives. I hate the question, "How are you?" It seems simple enough, and those who ask it have only the best intentions. But here's the thing: You're asking me to do all the work. And that is an energy suck. I need people to jump on board the train and be all-in, which means keeping up with my social media and being up-to-speed enough to know the major items happening in my life. Anyone else just has to go in the acquaintance category. So when I text someone or I know that they are going through a tough time, it's my job as a friend to relieve their burden. That means showing up with dinner, sending a gift, or asking specific questions, like "How did that job interview go?"

I hate small talk. I physically cannot talk about the weather at length, and when someone does ask me, "How are you?" I typically respond with, "What would you like to know?" My soul rejects anything that isn't efficient or direct. I'm repulsed by wasting time; and anything I do, any interaction I have, and any conversation I engage in is going to mean something.

One of the most valuable lessons I learned from Gary V. is the importance of having one-on-one conversations. That means speaking directly to your target audience. He taught us that lesson in terms of social media. For example, when pushing out social media posts, target them to a person as if you ran into that person on the street. How would you talk to him or her? That's how the post should sound. For companies utilizing social media ads, have one targeted to moms who love dogs, one targeted to teenagers, and so forth. People react when they feel like they're being directly spoken to. So when you're having conversations with those in your life, go the extra mile to show them that you care through your questions and interactions.

In fact, the key to relationships is how you make other people feel. I often say that I think the biggest game-changer in our world would be if we first *thought* about how our actions might impact those around us instead of simply acting on what we want to do or say. We'd all be so much better off and have a much gentler, kinder, and mentally healthier world.

I tell you all of this because your mental well-being and relationships are the biggest factors to your happiness in both your personal and professional lives. To have any shot of being happy in your career, you have to make sure you've eliminated any energy vampires in your life.

So when I was deciding what was going to be next in my career, I knew one thing for certain: I was going to fill my days solely with good things and good people. And since I've made that decision, I've reached levels of happiness I didn't know were possible. It's all about eliminating the toxicity.

When it comes to your career journey, **you are the first you**. There are no wrong moves here and no precedent for how to do it right. Oscar Wilde is responsible for one of my absolute favorite quotes: "Be yourself; everyone else is already taken."

I'm someone who doesn't believe in competition, because we're all different and running our own races. I also likely feel that way because I don't believe in strangers. I just see them as unmet friends. I love people, and I believe that everyone has an interesting life story. If you don't think so, you're asking the wrong questions. Still, I actually need quite a bit of alone time and am an introvert in a lot of ways, especially in terms of recharging. But I get the biggest thrill in learning about people's life stories.

Gary taught us that, to be the best, you have two choices: you can build the biggest building or try and knock down all the other buildings around you. The first option is actually the only true success. You get nowhere and end up alone when you spend your life trying to compete and bring down those around you. As Gary says, legacy over currency.

My mom often gives the reminder to stay in your own lane. You can't control other people—only your own journey.

Also, do not tie your self-worth to a job. You have to be the exact same, whole person whether you're working or you're not, because superficial and outside factors can change at any time. So don't let them define you, or you're going to take a big blow when those chapters come to an end.

So I tuned out everyone and everything around me and acknowledged what truly made my heart the happiest. And the answer was that my soul wanted to be in Tampa and get to see family all the time. I didn't want to have to pick and choose what holidays and family events I attended. I craved being at *all* of them. I wanted to be in the city I love, surrounded by water, sunshine, and warm weather. Peace out, winter.

I also never understood why, with all the different types of people and personalities we have on this planet, everyone has the same work schedule. Why is a typical workday Monday through Friday from approximately nine a.m. to five p.m. with a one-hour lunch, *if you are lucky*? Who decided this rule? The same person who also decided you couldn't wear white after Labor Day?

If you couldn't tell, I'm not into monotony to start with, and I certainly never loved or embraced Mr. Dictatorial's robotic work schedule that every human must follow.

I'm a big believer in finding the schedule that works for your soul. That was another big factor I wanted in this next chapter of my life. I love to travel. If I wanted to go to Africa or Thailand or leave early on Friday to go to a family wedding, I wanted to be able to do it. I am always going to remember those moments and trips with my family so much more than I would that day at the office. We get *one* life, and I didn't want to waste it missing out on what my heart wanted. Also, if I need to go to a doctor appointment in the middle of the day, I really don't want to ask permission. I will work whatever hours it takes to get the job done. I work plenty at night and on the weekends, and I don't mind if it means I get to take care of my life priorities during the day.

I often hear the debate, especially among working women, about how to achieve work-life balance. The answer is that *it does not exist*. You just have to address whatever is most pressing at the moment. Sometimes this means working during "off" hours, and sometimes, it's taking care of personal items during the day. But if we always prioritize whatever is most pressing at the moment, we're going to be much healthier and feel so much more at ease about the work-life-balance dynamic because we've addressed what our souls need the most at any given time.

I wanted to finally be able to completely fly and execute all the ideas that were tugging at my gut, which meant being my own boss. I really wanted to give it a chance and see what happened if I could fully realize and execute the ideas that were pulling at me and in the ways in which I wanted to do things. I wanted to be able to say no when someone was toxic or treating me less than the way I deserved. I wanted to see what happened if I could do the work I loved and that I'd had so much success with, but without the often-toxic workplace politics.

We have to realize that perfection does not exist. Stop trying to chase it.

What is perfection, anyway? No one can pinpoint it. Success comes from what you make of a situation and the confidence behind it. For example, there's no perfect name out there for a company. Successful companies became big names because of their results and their impact on the world. The closest you can get to success is by knowing your gut so well that you have an unwavering belief in yourself and the decisions you make. I have people come up to me all the time and tell me they think that Social Victories is a perfect name and that they love it. I literally made it up. In my head. But it's become mainstream with everyone who knows me and for my clients *because of what it's become.*

You often have to take the first step, or leap of faith, before anyone else can see it. So when it comes time for the next step in your life, write down the three passions your heart needs the most. Also consider what deal-breakers you won't accept. Then pick a job based on those factors.

Which is exactly what I did.

Based on all the criteria I just named, I decided to give up a steady paycheck and go full time with Social Victories. *Gulp.*

## Chapter Lessons

- Your highest level of happiness will be reached when you commit to allowing zero percent toxicity in your life.
- If anyone makes you feel less than what you deserve, they are likely not an equal.
- If you don't stand up for yourself, who will?
- If you consistently feel net negative about a relationship or work dynamic at the end of every day, it means there is something better out there for you.
- People will do what you allow them to do.
- Getting rid of toxic people in your life is addition by subtraction.
- Authentic people's actions exactly match how they're feeling inside.
- One-on-one conversations are the most effective way of communicating to elicit a response from your target audience.
- Don't make permanent decisions based on temporary people.
- There is only one answer that means yes, and that is yes. If the answer is *no, I'm not sure, maybe,* or *I'm not ready,* the answer is currently no.
- Your mental well-being is too big a price to pay.
- Pay attention to people's actions, not just their words. People are their actions.
- If we first thought about how our actions might affect those around us instead of doing what we want to do or say, our world would be a much better place.
- Fill your days with good things and good people.
- Everyone has an interesting life story, and if you don't think so, you're asking the wrong questions.
- To be the best, build the biggest building. Don't waste your time trying to knock down all the buildings around you.

- No one says you have to work Monday through Friday, nine a.m. to five p.m. Find a schedule that works for your soul.
- Work-life balance is about addressing whatever is most pressing at the moment.
- Perfection doesn't exist. Stop trying to chase it.
- Success is knowing yourself so well that you have an unwavering belief in who you are and the decisions you make.
- You have to take the first step, or leap of faith, before anyone else can see it.

# CHAPTER 11

# SOCIAL VICTORIES

You never know who needs your help until you let people know you're available to assist. I was grateful I'd done the work to build the foundation of Social Victories on the side while I was making a full-time salary elsewhere. The key word that comes to mind when building a business is *sacrifice*.

It was now January of 2018, and since the summer of 2016, I'd been building out different parts of my company as I'd earn money and when I had free time. In fact, almost all of my free time went to working on the business. I had to make major sacrifices in other parts of my life, but I still committed to never miss anything familywise or any event that was really important to me.

During that time period, from when I first launched the company in 2016 to the beginning of 2018, I'd completed all of the necessary paperwork done to become an official company, I'd grabbed all of the social media handles, and I'd had the website built—just the basics. But when it came time to go out on my own full time, I had all the pieces in place—all I had to do was share them. I remember that I made the decision to go full time the second week of January in 2018. I spent the next day thinking, *What did I just do?* (and probably eating pizza and ice cream all day), but I shared my website and social media handles publicly and officially let people know I was available to help full-time. From basically the next day on, I was busy nonstop. I couldn't believe the number of people responding to me, letting me know they needed assistance. I would've never known that these people or companies needed social media and marketing help if I hadn't told them I had a business that could assist.

When I first launched the business I had some hesitation before going all in. I was worried because I didn't have experience executing social media ads, which are a large part of the social media world. I'd only watched my colleagues at Vayner do the execution, although I knew the general premise of what the ads could achieve. I could talk about them and their importance, but I'd never actually been the one to bring them to life. I told Paul Sickmon, whose company Knox Sports was one of my first clients, that I could help them with social media strategy and best practices. But I'd have to bring in someone else to help with the ads side of things, as they were the main revenue driver on social media at the time, and I hadn't had experience implementing them yet. He gave me a very important piece of advice: don't underestimate yourself.

Paul believed in me and my capabilities and had no doubt I could execute those ads. So I trusted him and dove right in. I spent time researching and practicing launching ads. And what do you know? After a pretty short amount of time, I was able to teach myself and grasp how to run ads on social. *I could do it, after all.* And now I had every capability I needed to fully launch the business. Paul believed in me before I completely believed in myself. It's so important to have people like that around you.

When I'm making a big decision, I have a tribe of people comprised of family and friends that I trust implicitly and turn to in order to help guide me on life's biggest decisions. They are also the people I lean on when I have good or bad news to share. As a group, they seem to always be right. Whenever I pose an important question to them, they are typically unanimous in knowing what's best for me. When I told "the tribe" that I was planning to go full-time with my own company, without missing a beat, every single one of them said that they knew it was going to be successful and that it was the obvious right decision for me to make. They helped erase any lingering doubt, and so I went full-steam ahead with Social Victories, knowing the tribe had a flawless track record of being right.

Within the first week of my full-time venture with Social Victories, I signed my first NFL player. Brandon Copeland saw the work I was doing for Brandon Marshall, as Cope (as we call him) worked out at Marshall's gym, where Cope's trainer Troy Jones was based. Cope and I started following each other on Instagram when I was working with Brandon Marshall. Then, after following each other for a while, we messaged back and forth one day, and Cope told me he'd watched the work I'd been doing with Brandon (you never know who's watching what you're doing!), and he was interested in some marketing help himself.

Cope was making a comeback from an injury and was with the Detroit Lions at the time. He'd spent the beginning of his career focusing on making teams and overcoming the adversity that the NFL throws your way. But in our first conversation, I knew he was something special and meant for real greatness. I can instantly tell when a person has the intangibles—they are comfortable and easy to talk to and exhibit the work ethic, loyalty, devotion, and down-to-earth nature that the greatest leaders possess. I couldn't believe how relatable and normal our first conversation was. We were on the same page about business, and it was like talking to a friend. I owe Brandon Copeland so much gratitude because he was the first NFL player who took a chance on me in my own business. I introduced him to as many people as I could who could possibly be an asset for him in the business world. One of those people was Gary Vaynerchuk, and the two of them recorded a podcast together. Not long afterward, Brandon signed with the Jets, so imagine Gary's joy and the fate of that introduction, as Gary is an absolute diehard Jets fan and often talks about buying the team one day. Those two have stayed in touch and have been a resource in business for one another since that meeting.

We slowly worked to build Brandon's brand, or his (Brand)on, as I guess we can call it. Step by step, he kindly trusted me to make any introduction I saw fit. (I love connecting people who are meant to know each other in the world and can make one another's lives so much better. It's one of my greatest joys in life.) Anyone I suggested he hop on the phone with, he did so without hesitation. I noticed that Brandon had a knack and passion for financial literacy, which was incredibly rare among NFL players. I suggested we tell the world about his area of expertise.

One of the first projects we did together was a partnership with the Players' Tribune. I'd let the Tribune know that Brandon was my client, he was local to the New York area, and he was willing to come into their office at any time. So they reached out and suggested we do a piece on Brandon's five main financial tips for incoming NFL rookies right before the Draft in 2018. From there, we started reaching out to get Brandon speaking opportunities at events and companies. The momentum started building. He then became a professor in the off-season at his alma mater, the University of Pennsylvania, where he taught a class called Life 101, which focused on financial literacy. And before you knew it, he was featured on every major media outlet as the NFL player who had a real estate flipping business and was the financial literacy guru in his "free time." The week of the NFL Draft in 2019, Brandon (who was undrafted at the beginning of his career) was the main story on ESPN's homepage. His off-the-field legacy helped his on-the-field opportunities, as teams are looking for the guy who is a winner on *and off* the field.

During the 2019 Super Bowl in Atlanta, I was working on landing another appearance for Cope, as I'd done for him at the 2018 Super Bowl in Minnesota. A ton of athletes were coming in for the big game that year, and it seemed like there were fewer sponsorship opportunities available compared to the year before. I reached out to a number of businesses in the Atlanta area and just couldn't find a speaking opportunity or appearance for Cope. He had his flight booked to Atlanta, but finally, the week of the Big Game, he canceled his ticket, as I had come up empty. I was so hard on myself and felt like such a failure. I cared about Cope and wanted to bring opportunities to life for him. I don't like failing, and not getting the job done is absolutely not in my DNA. I had tears in my eyes, I was so upset that I couldn't deliver for him.

But even when there's no chance of making something happen, I *still* don't give up.

I did some more research and kept Googling all the events happening at the Super Bowl that year. I finally found out there was a Panini autograph table at the NFL Experience. Thanks to the guidance of my lifelong friend, Jamie Grant, who worked at the NFLPA (National Football League Players Association), I was able to reach out to the guy running the Panini activation at NFL Experience. I'm so grateful for all Jamie has done to help with Social Victories. I emailed the contact and didn't hear back. So I called him at work. I still didn't hear back. Of course I didn't. It was the week of the Super Bowl— *which meant he wasn't at his desk!*

Then, on my flight to Atlanta the Wednesday before the Super Bowl, I reached out to another friend who worked at the NFL offices, and she was able give me his cell number. I texted him, and he texted back and told me all the slots at the autograph table were filled. But turns out, he was from Tampa and was a really nice guy. We totally hit it off over text!

The next day, Thursday afternoon, I received a text from him saying that they'd just had a cancellation at the autograph table and asking if Brandon could be in Atlanta on Saturday by five p.m. I couldn't believe it! That hustle and relentless effort *had* paid off. I basically said that he would absolutely take it. I called Brandon, and he couldn't believe it, either. He booked his flight, and a car service was waiting for him at the airport when he arrived. His appearance included him sitting in the middle of the NFL Experience, in front of a packed room of thousands and thousands of fans, signing autographs for them. He was also featured on the big screen above the stage, and there was a constant stream of fans, for two hours straight, waiting for his autograph. Additionally, he got paid more than we ever expected to get for an appearance that week. And that's an example of how we started from nothing and have built our way up.

I could never do what I do with this business without the guys I work with. They are my champions, and they took a chance on someone who looked completely different from them and was just starting out. Finding champions who are totally different from you is so important because you can open doors for each other that the other one can't. For the athletes I work with, they are able to give me access and provide the most coveted stage on the planet. I, on the other hand, can share my business expertise with them and help them acclimate to life in their city and off the field, as well as prepare them for life after sports.

I always tell my clients that the best way to build a brand is to figure out who you are authentically and what makes you different from everyone else in the world. Once we hone in on the three or four pillars that make *you the first you*, those become our content buckets. We then focus on amplifying those facets of their personality to the world. In order to successfully build a brand, people must understand *you* first. You're never going to support or vouch for someone you don't understand or connect with. And the way to get people to understand you is simplicity and consistency. Select those few traits that set you apart from everyone else in the world and go all in on those aspects of your personality. Consistently practice them, which should be easy to do if the traits you selected are authentically you. Over time, that repetition will begin to resonate with fans, and they will understand who you are and what you stand for. For example, people in my life know I love Tampa, traveling, food, sports, my family, and pets, because those are the things I constantly post and talk about. If we look at LeBron James, his brand has become so big because people understand who he is, as he's consistent with his behaviors and passions. He loves basketball and his family, and he started the I Promise School.

He talks about those categories constantly, so fans have come to learn them well over time. Similarly, each of my athlete clients has a niche off the field that sets him or her apart from everyone else.

Shortly after I signed Cope, I began getting requests to be a guest on podcasts and to start giving speeches and appearing at conferences. I documented everything I did on social media so that people knew what I was up to and would consider me for opportunities. When I was at MLB, my contact at the Chicago Cubs was Mary Reisert. She always stood out to me as someone who was stellar at her job and an even higher quality person. We stayed in touch over the years, and as she saw me launch my business, she had since joined IBM. Mary reached out to me and told me that IBM was looking to bring a handful of social media influencers to its annual Think conference in 2018 in Las Vegas, and she asked if I would be interested in being one of them. Um . . . *absolutely!*

She submitted me as a candidate, and I was selected! I already thought I'd hit the jackpot in being chosen, but this experience was about to get a whole lot better. Mary let me know that, as an influencer, I had an opportunity to have my headshot taken and be featured on a screen at the conference. I thought, *Hey, it can never hurt to have a fresh headshot; let's go for it!* I went through my photo shoot and interview, answering a few brief questions, and then went on my way. That night, I received an email with the subject line "See yourself at 18,600 sq. ft." I thought, *I should probably open this.*

And there was my headshot on the most massive billboard I have ever seen, along with a quote I'd given during the interview. I figured that if I'd ended up on a screen that huge, it must be in the middle of nowhere. But when I looked at the address in the email, it had the billboard sitting *right in the middle of the Las Vegas Strip.*

I couldn't wrap my head around the possibility that my photo was that large in the middle of the Vegas Strip. I walked out of my hotel and, sure enough, I could see myself halfway down the Strip. The photo was up there for five days. It was one of the wildest moments of my life. And it's a reminder that the best opportunities come from building quality relationships. Mary was my peer at the time. So many people are focused on networking up, but networking to the side is just as important—if not *more* important—as people want to help out people they like.

I could never have anticipated the billboard experience, but each little win helped the company grow over time. That appearance was the first moment I really thought, *I am going to be okay in this business*. And, by the way, IBM invited me back the next year (thanks again to Mary), and I was once again on a billboard—but this time, in San Francisco. So I like to think I'm a billboard professional at this point.

Shortly after I returned from Las Vegas, a guy named Ryan Hill, who I'd just gone to lunch with in the Tampa community, reached out to me on Twitter and told me he'd just heard a Tampa Bay Buccaneers player on the radio talking about how he'd been searching for a marketing person for a while. Ryan, knowing what I did, asked if he could connect us and reached out on my behalf to see if the Bucs player would be interested in talking with me. As a kid who grew up a die-hard Bucs fan and made a scrapbook when they won the Super Bowl, *was this really happening?* I felt like I was in a dream. The Bucs player's name was Cameron Lynch. Little did I know at that moment how much Cam would change my life. We talked a bit on Twitter, then got to know each other over the phone, and finally decided to meet at a restaurant in Tampa. Cam often talks about how I was wearing a colorful dress and I ordered a pizza and basically ate the whole thing myself (so many great moments in my life have happened while eating pizza!). Cam later told me he felt very comfortable with me, and my eating capabilities reminded him of his fellow teammates in the locker room. *My mom would be so proud.*

Cam is the most outgoing, positive, and loving person you could ever meet. We hit the ground running. Cam was my first Tampa athlete, so he will always hold a special place in my heart. I attended the Bucs games each week and was able to see my client playing on the field. It was a true thrill. I'd capture videos of him, and he became a mainstay on the JumboTron at Raymond James Stadium for his energy and dancing skills during games. We visited veterans who'd been wounded in combat at a Wounded Warriors Abilities Ranch in the Tampa Bay area, and we began creating partnership and endorsement opportunities, as well. Cam was selected to broadcast the Super Bowl by the NFL in 2019 and took me with him for the week. Cam was one of the first people in my life to show me what I deserve. That Super Bowl in Atlanta, I had two clients with appearances. I felt like a real agent and that we'd made so much progress as a business, considering I now had two NFL players featured on the biggest stage. It was a real moment of legitimacy for me.

I also came to realize throughout the course of working with these guys that a lot of athletes have help getting to the pros, but no one helps them maximize their time in the spotlight, acclimate to the new cities they're in, or assist them with building a life after pro sports, which could end at any moment. I cared too much about these guys to see them left high and dry, and it became my mission to better their lives. Even if you're the fourth-string punter on the team, people will meet with you because you're a celebrity to them. But the minute your career ends, you become a moot point. So that means we need to work quickly.

In addition, athletes have agents, and teams have digital and social media departments, but it didn't seem like anyone was proactively helping athletes build their brands and futures off the field. So that's where I came in. Because he lived in Tampa, Cam became like family. He came to our house for Thanksgiving, and we eventually launched a podcast together, called Energy Captains, where we talk about building brands in the sports world. My family becomes family to my athletes, and their families become mine. The best strategy in life is caring, and it's all about trust on both sides.

Cam is incredibly passionate and talented when it comes to broadcasting. During our time working together, Cam has landed many major broadcasting opportunities and hosting roles. He also launched a media company of which he is the CEO. While so many guys wonder, *What will I do tomorrow?* when their professional sports careers come to an end—which can really affect their mental well-being—Cam gets to choose the path he wants to pursue. He has already become an entrepreneur with a conglomerate of business entities and pathways, and I feel really good about that.

I am only doing about 50 percent of what I thought I'd do when I started my business. I first started out thinking I was just going to be helping athletes with social media guidance and possibly endorsement deals. And then their needs became greater, and I was open to what they threw my way. It's so important to keep your finger on the pulse of how your business is evolving and to monitor the needs of your clients. I like to say that I collect good people and take them with me everywhere. I met my graphic-design partner, Michael Scott, in a previous job and loved his character, so when it came time to build my own business, I wanted to give him all of my graphic-design work, as he was the best person I knew and the best in his field.

I never expected to offer all the services I do today, but when the need came about, if I could add them to my offerings, I did. It's important to be open and say yes when you have the capability to add a skill set to your company.

Like when Cam had me renovate his house.

I connected Cam to a friend who's a Realtor and could help him purchase a house in Tampa. One day, he had me come over after practice to help him pick out tile. Then I selected the carpet . . . and the paint . . . and then the wood for the stairs. The next thing I knew, he was headed to scrimmage the Tennessee Titans for nine days, the renovations were beginning, and I was the one overseeing them. We often laugh about the time the contractors called to tell me a toilet upstairs was leaking and if they didn't get it stopped, it was going to flood the house overnight. *How was I going to make that call to Cam to tell him I'd flooded his entire house while he was away?* Luckily, they were able to figure it out.

Now I say that my role is to help my clients become the best versions of themselves. In fact, Cam calls me Corporate Mom. I used to think I'd be at a disadvantage, being a younger female in the field, and I look completely opposite of what a traditional NFL representative looks like. But I came to realize that a lot of my clients were raised by single moms. So in their minds, *women get the job done.* My nurturing personality and nature actually gave me a leg up, as the guys were missing that motherly taste of home in the NFL. Most of these guys are still in their twenties, and they're thrust into adulthood in a big way, which can be lonely at times. Cam and I often say of one another that the other person is who we'd want to go to battle with. You're going to have trials and tribulations in life and business, and you need to partner with people who support you and are at their best when you're at your worst. I feel that way about all of my clients, and it's what has made Social Victories such a joyful and fulfilling chapter in my life.

In 2018, I was selected as one of fifty ambassadors from around the country to participate in an all-expenses-paid trip to Denver Startup Week, another opportunity I could've never imagined. My second year of business, 2019, was the year I completed a certificate in women's entrepreneurship from Cornell University, became a certified marketing agent by the NFLPA, and signed on to work with two sports leagues as clients. One of my former bosses at MLB, Dinn Mann, brought me out to speak to the AAF, or Alliance of American Football, during its first and only training camp. I got to go room to room, speaking to each team on social media and branding. It was basically the first time I'd ever presented to entire rooms full of athletes and teams as a whole. Many of those guys went back to the NFL and other pro football leagues and have stayed in touch to this day. It was a great opportunity for exposure and to grow my business. The next step on the ladder. I could have never predicted so many of these opportunities that have come to fruition, but it's a matter of being great at what you do, giving your all every day, and documenting your journey so that you're front of mind for opportunities. You never know who's watching!

I signed two more NFL players, Hakeem Valles and Steve McLendon. Each has his specific and inspiring niche off the field. More importantly, they are two of the greatest guys I've ever met—both in personality and character. I feel lucky that this business is filled with the best people on the planet, and I truly get to honor my wish of filling my days with only good things and good people. The NFL guys I work with make me a better person.

People give me unsolicited advice all the time about my company and how I should run it and grow it. I know exactly why I started my business and what I want it to become. I also know best what my soul needs on a daily basis. So the bigger the venture you have, the more tunnel vision you need to have. You know why you began a journey in the first place. Do not let the peanut gallery influence or derail you from what's best for you. Remember, *you are the first you!*

## CHAPTER LESSONS

- You never know who needs your help until you let them know you're available.
- A major key to building a business is sacrifice.
- Don't underestimate what you're capable of achieving.
- Find a tribe of people you can trust implicitly and that you can rely on when making major life decisions.
- It's a cliché, but you never know who's watching your work. Always keep that hope alive that you're being noticed by the right people without even realizing it.
- Find champions who are different than you, who can open up doors that you can't. Together, you make a great team.
- The best way to build a brand is to select a few pillars that make you authentically you and then practice those behaviors over and over so that people can understand what makes *you the first you.*

- Document all that you are doing in your business so that people know all that you're up to and will think of you for opportunities.
- Network to the side—with peers—instead of just focusing on networking "up." In business, people want to help out and work with people they like.
- Businesses are built slowly over time. Every win you have helps grow your overall reputation.
- The best strategy in life is caring.
- Collect good people and take them with you everywhere.
- In work and personal relationship dynamics, make sure you choose people you can go to battle with and come out stronger on the other side.

# CHAPTER 12

# FULL CIRCLE

If there's one thing I know for sure since I started this business, it's that I didn't know this level of happiness was possible. Coming up with my non-negotiables of living in Tampa, making my own schedule, being able to execute my own ideas and go with my gut were game-changers for me. I encourage you to write down your list, as well, and follow it with all of your heart.

It's amazing where following your heart can lead you. Not only has mine brought me to happiness, but it's also brought me full circle. I shared in the beginning of the book how my dad grew up dreaming of living in a condo and having the glamorous lifestyle of the Yankees heroes he grew up idolizing. As I write this book, I'm coincidentally living out my dad's dream: I now live in a condo, and a New York Yankees player lives in my building. A major joy throughout my career in sports has been making my dad proud, and everything I can do to honor his passions—including working for MLB—puts a smile on my face. Life is amazing!

Your greatest happiness is out there for you. All you have to do is follow your heart, tune out the noise, and go *be the first you!*

CHAPTER LESSON

# YOU ARE THE FIRST YOU

# ACKNOWLEDGMENTS

I am forever grateful to my family for all of their support and excitement as I wrote this book. This entire journey wouldn't have been possible without them. My parents, Gail and Steve, are my heroes. They've allowed me to be exactly who I am throughout my entire life, which is the greatest gift they could've ever given me. They have enthusiastically fostered and supported the unique person that I am. My journey detailed in this book wouldn't have been possible if they hadn't been there to catch me when I fell and to be my biggest cheerleaders when the most exciting moments happened in my life. A huge shout-out to my brother, Josh, who makes our family whole and who is my teammate in life. His support and excitement for this project meant so much, and he inspires so many with his intelligence, big heart, and his own unique journey.

I owe my dad, Steve, the biggest debt of gratitude for not only being the best dad, but also for being the lawyer for Social Victories and all of my business needs. There are so many questions and issues that come up on a daily basis. I couldn't follow my dreams and run Social Victories if it weren't for my dad helping me with all the legal questions and paperwork I have to tackle. He's such a hero for all the work he's done to help me, and he does it out of the goodness of his heart. Dad, thanks for saving the day when I call you with all of my pressing and last-minute questions!

I am so appreciative of all my friends who understood that writing this book took up almost all of my free time for months, and I didn't have as much time to see them as I normally would. When I'd let them know it was another night or week of book writing, they came back with cheers of support for the project as a whole and fully understood why I was booked (no pun intended). I'm so appreciative of everyone in my life who made sacrifices to make this book possible and for everyone who was a cheerleader of mine throughout this entire journey. I'm so grateful for my tribe. I don't know what I'd do without you all! An extra shout-out goes to David Moskovitz. I had surgery in the middle of writing this book, and my computer broke right afterward, as I was beginning my recovery. David brought me his computer to use so that I could keep writing. Chapter 6 was written on his computer, and the book would've gone from chapter 5 to chapter 7 without him ☺, so I'm grateful for his selflessness and act of generosity! I am also so appreciative of everyone who offered to read the book along the way. Knowing I had my tribe behind me, whom I trust with all of my heart and who were willing to selflessly sacrifice their own time to help me, made me feel so supported and put me at ease.

Finally, thank you to the Indigo Publishing Team who believed in me as an author before I ever imagined the idea for myself. I am so appreciative of Alicia Grubb, who first found me and believed that my journey was a story to tell and could be a guide to help others. I'll never forget our first phone conversation, and major props to Alicia for strongly believing we need more books by female entrepreneurs out there. This journey would truly not have been possible without the green light from Indigo's CEO, Dan Vega. Dan is one of the few people who understands me better than I could ever describe myself. Thank you for comprehending my soul so deeply and believing in the person that I am. During all of our conversations, you let me be 100 percent me and made me feel so comfortable. What a gift! I also cannot thank you enough for green-lighting this project. I'm really excited to have written a book! It changed my life forever. And a MAJOR thank you to my editor, Liesel Schmidt. I am so grateful to Liesel for truly being there day in and day out (we talked basically every day) during the entire writing process. Not only did Liesel support me in letting me get every ounce of what I thought was important into the book, she made each chapter better and, very quickly, she became a friend. Liesel, I couldn't have gone through this process without you. Thank you for believing in my story and sharing your own. You are such a special part of this book, and you are the reason my first book has ever come to life! I'm so happy to have made another friend during this process who understands and supports me. There were many people at Indigo who read this book and put their personal touches on it to make it better. Thank you so much to Regina Cornell for going through my book with a fine-toothed comb. You are an editing genius! I'm also so grateful to Jackson Haynes and Bobby Dunaway, who quarterbacked this book process.

To anyone who reads this book: We've only got one life, and I hope yours is filled with an unwavering belief in yourself and the greatest happiness possible. Whenever you start to feel doubt about who you are, please imagine me sending you a hug and reminding you that you can't mess this up—*you are the first you!*

This book is dedicated to everyone who has ever believed in me.

# ABOUT THE AUTHOR

Whitney Holtzman is a passionate go-getter and the CEO of Social Victories, a social media and marketing consulting company for leaders in the sports world. Her passion has always been at the intersection of sports and giving back, and she helps her clients across pro sports build their brands and become the best versions of themselves. Prior to her role representing players, Whitney built her career in sports, marketing, and social media at espnW, Major League Baseball, VaynerMedia, and RISE (Ross Initiative in Sports for Equality), which uses the power of sports to unite neighborhoods and advocate for racial equality.

Whitney grew up in Tampa, Florida, (a city she loves) and is an avid sports fan, thanks to her dad, who made Monday Night Football a staple in the Holtzman household. She attended the University of Florida during the Tebow era and experienced two football championships and a basketball title during her time as a Gator. In college, Whitney interned for the Tampa Bay Rays, Turner Sports, and ESPN. She is an avid traveler who hopes to visit every state and continent. Whitney is also the only non-lawyer in her family, but she is excited to have found her passion at the intersection of sports and making the world a better place. Her greatest love is her family.